M000189429

The Q Guide to

Sex and the City

The Q Guides

FROM ALYSON BOOKS

AVAILABLE NOW:

POP CULTURE

Q

OUT THERE

GUIDE

The Q Guide to

Sex and the City

Stuff You Didn't Even Know You Wanted to Know ... about Carrie, Samantha, Miranda, and Charlotte ... and Cosmos

[**Robb Pearlman**]

a alyson books
N E W Y O R K

For David

MANUFACTURED IN THE UNITED STATES OF AMERICA

PUBLISHED BY ALYSON BOOKS
245 WEST 17TH STREET
NEW YORK, NY 10011

DISTRIBUTION IN THE UNITED KINGDOM BY
TURNAROUND PUBLISHER SERVICES LTD.
UNIT 3, OLYMPIA TRADING ESTATE
COBURG ROAD, WOOD GREEN,
LONDON N22 6TZ ENGLAND

FIRST EDITION: JUNE 2008

08 09 10 11 12 13 14 15 16 17 **a** 10 9 8 7 6 5 4 3 2 1

ISBN: 1-59350-072-6
ISBN-13: 978-1-59350-072-6

LIBRARY OF CONGRESS CATALOGING-IN-PUBLICATION DATA
ARE ON FILE.

COVER DESIGN BY VICTOR MINGOVITS
COVER ART BY WWW.GLENHANSON.COM.

Contents

Introduction

We couldn't help but
wonder . . .
Why a Q Guide to *Sex and
the City?*

THERE WAS a time when names like Carrie, Samantha,
Miranda, and Charlotte were just *names*. But now, especially when mentioned in the same breath, or breath-
less whisper, they carry not only the memory of one of
the most heralded television shows in history, but the
undeniable and inescapable aura of a fierce femininity,
independence, and balls-out sexuality, clothed in D&G,
shod in Manolos, and accessorized in Chanel.

And *Sex and the City*, the television show through
which these four characters entered our living rooms—
and bedrooms—on Sunday nights for years, has itself
become much more than *just* a television show. It has
morphed into nothing short of a phenomenon, conquering television as well as nearly every other aspect of

American popular culture. And of course, nothing can even get within arm's length of popular culture without getting the QSA: the Queer Stamp of Approval.

Let's face it, culturally and aesthetically, as go the gays, so goes the nation. We gentrify the neighborhoods. We pick the next season's must-haves before the current season is even under way. And where would people like Madonna, Cher, and yes, even little Britney, be without us? As Samantha says in Season Six, "First come the gays, then the girls, then the industry!"

And the industry came. The show won seven of its more than fifty Primetime Emmy® Award nominations and eight of the twenty-four Golden Globes for which it was nominated over its six seasons.

Selected Awards and Honors

1999
Women in Film: Lucy Award

2000
American Women in Radio & Television: Gracie Allen
    Award
Golden Globe® Award: Best Television Series
Golden Globe® Award: Best Actress: Sarah Jessica
    Parker

2001
Primetime Emmy® Award: Outstanding Comedy Series
American Women in Radio & Television: Gracie Allen
    Award
Columbus International Film & Video Festival for

Excellence in Costume Design Contemporary
Television

Golden Globe® Award: Best Television Series

Golden Globe® Award: Best Actress: Sarah Jessica
Parker

Makeup Artist and Hair Stylist Guild Award: Best
Makeup

Makeup Artist and Hair Stylist Guild Award: Best Hair
Styling

Producers Guild Golden Laurel Award

Screen Actors Guild Award: Outstanding Actress: Sarah
Jessica Parker

TV Cares: Ribbon of Hope Award

2002

Primetime Emmy® Award: Outstanding Direction:
Michael Patrick King

Primetime Emmy® Award: Outstanding Casting:
Jennifer McNamara

Primetime Emmy® Award: Outstanding Costumes:
Patricia Field, Rebecca Weinberg

Golden Globe® Award: Best Television Series

Golden Globe® Award: Best Actress: Sarah Jessica Parker

American Women in Radio and Television: Gracie
Allen Award

Producers Guild Award

Screen Actors Guild Award: Outstanding Performance
by an Ensemble

2003

American Women in Radio and Television: Gracie
Allen Award

Primetime Emmy® Award: Outstanding Casting:
  Jennifer McNamara
Golden Globe® Award: Best Performance by a Support-
  ing Actress: Kim Cattrall
Makeup Artist and Hair Stylist Guild Awards: Best Hair
  Styling

2004
Primetime Emmy® Award: Outstanding Lead Actress:
  Sarah Jessica Parker
Primetime Emmy® Award: Outstanding Supporting
  Actress: Cynthia Nixon
Golden Globe® Award: Best Actress: Sarah Jessica
  Parker
Screen Actors Guild Award: Outstanding Ensemble

We should be proud, really. Because thanks to our knack of spotting a winner much earlier than anyone else (as well as the critical acclaim, strong ratings, incredible marketing campaign, and just plain old quality programming), *Sex and the City quickly made its way into American popular culture, and doesn't show any sign of vacating its spot on the cultural landscape. Tons of shows still reference and parody the show. For ex*ample, in the "Nookie in New York" episode of *The Simpsons*, it is described as being about "four women who act like gay men," while its Sunday-night Fox neighbor, *Family Guy*, described it as being about "three hookers and their mom." The show's demise was mourned by Karen and Jack on *Will & Grace*'s "No Sex 'N the City" episode, while the inmates of HBO's

Oz lamented their inability to watch the girls without cable television.

Luckily, Carrie, Samantha, Miranda, and Charlotte aren't going anywhere. And neither is New York. So sit back, pour yourself a Cosmopolitan, and get ready. Is this the Q *Guide* for you? Absofuckinlutely.

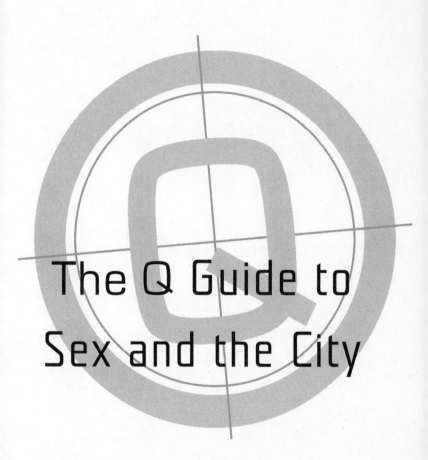

The Q Guide to
Sex and the City

CHAPTER ONE

The Book

QUOTE

We couldn't help but wonder . . .
Does source material count as foreplay?

CANDACE BUSHNELL'S "Sex and the City" first appeared in 1994 as a column in *The New York Observer.* A single woman's view of relationships, dating, and sex, it was the first column to celebrate, as well as illuminate the state of the modern urban woman"—or, at the very least, the fashionable, successful, party-going, recreational drug-using, modernly post-modern woman. Bushnell chronicled the experiences of New Yorkers as they led their aspirational, if not inspirational, lives in the heady days of the mid-1990s. Bushnell's subjects lived in the same New York as her readers. And though her readers might have never gone to (or have been let in to) the same hot spots as her characters did, they were, more importantly, having similar romantic and sexual experiences in their own lives. Let's face it, if you're getting dumped at three in the morning, it doesn't matter if it's happening over a $15 martini in SoHo or a five dollar draught in Flushing.

A brief note about New York City at this time in history might be necessary for those who either weren't here to experience it or those who, for reasons they know all too well, simply can't remember it. This was a New York like none other. Run for the first time in years, and for reasons nobody could quite wrap their heads around, by a Republican mayor who, depending on your perspective, either cleaned up or destroyed the soul of the city. The homeless miraculously, if not somewhat suspiciously, disappeared from the streets. Times Square's porn shops and theaters were torn down to build a family-friendly enclave of chain restaurants and cartoon-themed musicals. The crime rate went down, the tourist trade went up, and New Yorkers were enjoying the benefits of the dot com boom, the surging of the stock market, neighborhood gentrification, and the long awaited, if still incomplete, resolution to the AIDS crisis.

Lo, the renaissance of the New York fashionista was upon us. And it was good.

When Bushnell's column first apperad, everyone was talking about it. Well, everyone in the five boroughs. It wasn't until 1997, when her columns were published in the book, *Sex and the City,* that her take on New Yorkers, and New York, gained mainstream acclaim. The book was called "sly" and "sharp" *by People* magazine. The *Los Angeles Times* called it "fascinating" and "hilarious," and went on to say "Welcome to the cruel planet that is Manhattan." A cross-country dig at New York? Perhaps, but all New Yorkers know that 1. LA is just jealous (let's face it, when you say "The City" to anyone—anyone—in the world, they're going to think New York), and 2. yes, Manhattan is a cruel planet. But it's ours, and if you can make it here, especially if you can make it with that cute guy from the bar, you can make it anywhere.

Just what Bushnell and her characters think of gays and lesbians becomes very clear, very early on in the book. In fact, Bushnell tells us about a gay man before even naming any of the central characters we've come to know. The section, "In Love at the Bowery Bar, Part 2," begins with the following:

> At my table at the Bowery Bar, there's Parker, thirty-two, a novelist who writes about relation-ships that inevitably go wrong; his boyfriend, Roger; Skipper Johnson, an entertainment lawyer.

Hold on a minute, did she just casually mention the fact that this Parker guy has a boyfriend? And this is a book that's reviewed, favorably, in *People*? The maga-zine that entire swaths of the country rely on for advice on what to do, read, and care about? And it's OK?

You had us at "relationships that inevitably go wrong," but this is too much, Ms. Bushnell. We offi-cially heart you.

Stanford Blatch, the character immortalized in the television series by actor Willie Garson, makes his first appearance in an equally casual manner in the chapter "Skipper and Mr. Marvelous Seek Hot Sex in Southhampton Hedges." The three "hopeful bachelors" featured in this chapter are each given a Dating Game (or for you Chuck Woolery fans, a Love Connection)–style introduction. Stanford, or in this case, "Bachelor No. 3" is described thus:

> Stanford Blatch, thirty-seven. Screenwriter. The next Joe Eszterhas. Gay but prefers straight guys. Long, dark, curly hair; refuses to cut it or put it in a ponytail.

OK, so Garson's not the first guy you think of to portray Stanford based on that description, but that's not the issue here. Bushnell, once again, gives us yet another "so what if he's gay?" moment. In the book, Stanford does wind up marrying a woman named Suzannah, (a theme which comes to the forefront of Season Five's season finale in which Nathan Lane's "isn't he gay?" Bobby marries, to everyone's surprise, Julie Halston's Bitsy). It's very clear, to Stanford, his bride-to-be, and the reader that they are entering into nothing more than a business arrangement. Yes, their friendship goes back many years, so the companionship will be nice, but the union is nevertheless based on the fact that by marrying, they will each be able to collect and share inheritances. Stanford and Suzannah's formal declaration of their need for separate bedrooms is treated not as a tragic consequence of bending to societal pressure, but as an incidental aside that adds to the overall comedy and absurdity of the situation.

And despite the fact that we've come to think of the

book as a treatise on the single straight woman, Stanford's sexuality and relationships are treated with no more or less importance, or comment, than those of any of the other characters. One of Bushnell's gifts— and high on the list of reasons millions have flocked to her and her writing—is that she refuses to judge any of her characters. Stanford's sexuality just isn't an issue for her, and therefore neither is it for the reader. Stanford's sexual preference is mentioned, as it would be in conversation in the vast majority of New York circles, neither in a whisper, nor a shout, without condescension, or judgment. And really, what else would you expect from The City which proudly claims such out sons and daughters as Truman Capote, Walt Whitman, Tony Kushner, Cherry Jones, Rosie O'Donnell, and City Councilwoman Christine Quinn? And don't even get me started on the straight crowds that embrace our Pride and Halloween parades.

Though the vast majority of "non-straight" content of the book centers on gay men, lesbianism makes an appearance as well. Some may balk at the short shrift lesbians received in the book, but consider for a moment that lesbianism, as with everything else in the book, is seen from the perspective of straight women. And in the world Bushnell and her straight women inhabit, they befriend, for the most part, other straight women and gay men. Take this passage, in which Carrie relates what her straight woman friend Alex tells her:

> I mean, I've never been with a woman . . . Maybe
> I'm the only one—but who hasn't said, "I wish I
> could be a lesbian just so I wouldn't have to deal

with men." But the funny thing is, my friend said being with a woman was so intense because you're both women in the relationship. You know how women always want to talk about everything? Well, imagine that times two. It's constant talking. About everything, until four in the morning. After a while, she has to leave and go back to a man because she can't take the talking.

Alex's friend's take on lesbianism was explored years later in Season Four of the television series when Samantha decided to give lesbian love a try with Maria, played by Sonia Braga. After the initial rush of excitement, and the discovery of female ejaculation, Maria's need for constant communication became too much for Samantha to bear.

When a straight male character mentions girl-on-girl action, it's with a fairly predictable bent. Tad, "forty-one, a golden-boy architect," is talking about threesomes and the seemingly-new trend of women propositioning other women:

Women physically represent more sensuality and more beauty . . . So it's easier for a man to fantasize about two women being together. Two men together is kind of a dry fantasy.

OK, so this is not exactly the most accurate or evolved view of lesbianism. It's definitely one of the more popular straight views, spoken by a straight character, as written by a straight author. But consider this: Bushnell talked about it. In fact, she talked about homosexuality, through the guise of her characters, in more than what is often labeled as "gay-friendly," but in a gay-positive, gay-who-gives-a-damn, and gay-yeah-I'll-try-that way. Even in the late' 90s, with *Will & Grace* on the air, wasn't this something? And really, doesn't Samantha's story, despite its being played for a laugh, say something true about the lesbian dynamic? We've all heard girls who like girls make similar jokes. Bushnell had the nerve to bring up the topic, to push the boundaries, and to get people talking.

Bushnell had a unique ability to honestly and accurately portray her characters and their situations, though when you consider that she based them on her and her girlfriends, you might say she just took the inside track. Saying that most of her friends were more like Samantha than any of the others, she personally related more to Carrie. Bushnell knew that it was this dynamic of the friendship between single women that could serve as the wellspring for the greater overall project. "All of a sudden there was a huge population of women in their twenties and thirties who were single. Married women usually don't like discussing their sex lives because they either feel a certain loyalty to their husbands or they don't want to admit that they didn't marry a stud. But for single women, these bonds of loyalty aren't there, so single women would get together and talk about their disastrous dating experiences."

And talk about those experiences they did.

The characters didn't stop talking about the pleasures and pitfalls of single life, even through the transition from the book to the TV show. The first of the four television characters to be named in the book is Charlotte.

Here, Charlotte is not the preppy, conservative art dealer we've come to know and love, but an English journalist. Samantha, a "fortyish movie producer" appears a bit later. And though she's not quite the self-assured queen of public relations we know from the series, her character is perhaps the most consistent from book to screen. Sam, as she's most often called in the book, is not only given a man's name, but she's also described, shortly after her introduction, as having made a choice to say "screw it" and have sex like a man. And to round out the fabulous foursome, it's only until after we meet Miranda,

SEX AND THE SIDEBAR

If there was one relationship in the series that always kept me on the edge of my seat, it was Carrie's relationship with Big. Maybe it's because I have been there, and am still there myself with a man I deeply care for and see a future with who is in and out of my life and never seems to go away. You always hope that *your* Big will someday realize that you are the one for him. To be honest, it was a huge relief when Big rescued Carrie in Paris, but realistically, that's a rare, if not impossible "real-life" Big outcome to a Big problem. *Sex and the City* helped validate, for all of us who have had a Big in our lives, all the emotions and drama that are inherently part of that kind of relationship. Hopefully, though, we'll all eventually wise up and come to the conclusion that Carrie's happy ending just makes for good TV.

—LM, Account Executive and Social Spitfire

"thirty-two, a cable exec," that we meet the character who becomes the linchpin of the television series, Bushnell's alter-ego, Carrie, "thirty-four, some kind of journalist."

In 2005, well after *Sex and the City* became the cultural juggernaut it is, Bushnell was quoted as saying "The big question in *Sex and the City* is why are there so many great single women and no great guys to go out with them and marry them. That question remains unanswered."

CHAPTER TWO

Season One

A NOTE *about the seasonal and episodic summaries in this Q Guide: Let's not kid ourselves. There are a host of other resources readily available with information regarding the plots, production notes, scene-by-scene breakdowns of each episode, and the ever-popular which-girl-are-you quizzes. But this is a Q Guide, and as such we give you the information that you're most interested in, the information you're actually willing to pay money for.*

And by that, we mean we give you the stuff you can use to your advantage at cocktail parties. What you'll find here are the quips and quotes guaranteed to get you a laugh, even when used out of context; trivia to score you serious smarty pants points; highlights of the particularly Q and Q-friendly themes and events of the show; and Q and Q-iconic guest stars that are sure to send your happy hour taffeta into a tussle. And, of course, you'll find a complete and comprehensive listing of the featured men of each and every episode, including the names of the other Q-friendly productions they've been in.

Episode One: "Sex and the City"

Q-tastic Trivia

As with any new series, it's pretty clear, especially in the first few episodes, that the show is stuck in some sort of creative dressing room, trying on many different styles in an effort to best highlight its assets. For example, this season features the main and supporting characters speaking directly to the camera as well as on-the-street interviews with "real" people. The documentary style, perhaps in a nod to HBO sister series *Real Sex*, doesn't last long. Neither do Carrie's cadre of straight male friends. We can only assume that the producers and writers realize that these characters' purpose, to provide the straight male perspective on relationships and life would be better served by having the viewers tune in to *Super Bowl Sunday*. These men, as lovely as they were, all but disappear by the middle of Season Two.

And one last note for the season. This is the first time when a character, albeit a supporting one, is not only obviously gay, but proudly so. Stanford Blatch, the one male friend of Carrie's who stays throughout the series' entire run, is an over-the-top, hilarious representation of our community.

Q-tastic Moments

Like all good stories or, to be more accurate, good fairy tales, the series starts its run with a voice-over by Carrie, uttering the time-honored and always exciting "Once upon a time . . ." and then dissolves, almost immediately, to a scene of drag queens cavorting at a party. Cheers are heard throughout the land as a nation of gays and lesbians realize that they are not watching their mother's sitcom.

Carrie asks her boy friend (not *boyfriend*) Skipper if he's sure he's not gay because he's "nice." Proof that we've got the market on nice cornered!

The Men

Character	Actor	Slept with	Notes	*You might know him from such gay-friendly films and shows as*
Stanford	Willie Garson		Carrie's fabulous best gay friend	
Skipper	Ben Weber		Nice guy Straight friend of Carrie's	*Kissing Jessica Stein, The Broken Hearts Club, The Mirror Has Two Faces, Six Feet Under*
Capote	Jeffrey Nordling	Samantha	Videotapes his sex	*And the Band Played On*
Kurt	Bill Sage	Carrie	The first, not the last	*Mysterious Skin, Glitter*
Big	Chris Noth		Will we ever know his name?	

"Q"-uotes

"Just go out and have sex like a man."—Samantha

"The only place where one can still find love and romance in New York is the gay community. It's straight love that's become closeted."—Stanford

---

Episode Two: "Models and Mortals"

Q-tastic Moment

In a world seemingly hell-bent on beauty and perfection, Stanford speaks for us all when he questions his own physical attractiveness. It's difficult for people to feel good about themselves—especially people who, due to societal pressure, prevailing standards, and ignorance, are part of a minority and already feel diminished and second-class. Luckily, we're able to rely on our friends, our inner resources, and shows like this to bolster our self-confidence and give us hope that things are changing for the better so we can not only feel good in our own skins, but good about our bodies as well.

"Q"-uotes

"What's *cute* compared to *supermodel*?"—Miranda

"How can anyone that gorgeous be straight?"
   —Stanford

The Men

Character	Actor	Slept with	Notes	You might know him from such gay-friendly films and shows as
Stanford				
Derek	Andrea Boccaletti	sleeps, but doesn't "sleep" with Carrie	Underwear model, Stanford's only client	54
Skipper				
Barcley	Gabriel Macht	Samantha	Modelizer, someone who only dates models	The Object of My Affection, The Spirit
Nick	Josh Pais		Modelizer, someone who only dates models	Little Manhattan (with Cynthia Nixon!)

Episode Three: "Bay of Married Pigs"

Q-tastic Moments

Samantha says "marrieds" are jealous of singles because they can have sex anytime, anywhere, with anybody. Is that a straight/gay analogy or what? How many times have we heard, especially from the Right, that they think we're too promiscuous? And, similarly, how many times have we heard that the strongest proponents of anti-equality legislation have been caught with their pants down?

The Men

Character	Actor	Slept with	Notes	You might know him from such gay-friendly films and shows as
Peter	David Healy		Husband of Carrie's friend. He meets Carrie, naked, in the hallway one morning while she's visiting them in the Hamptons. He's described as being the same size as a peppermill.	
Sean	Scott Rabinowitz		A man incredibly intent on getting married, he sabotages every relationship, including the one he's having with Carrie.	
Tommy	Karl Geary	Samantha	Charlotte's Irish doorman who sleeps with drunk Samantha after Peter's all-marrieds party	

Miranda is set up on a blind date at her law firm's softball game with Syd (Joanna Adler). It's assumed that because she's single, she must be a lesbian, and if there are two single lesbians within six feet of one another, people will set them up because really, why wouldn't they work as a couple? It's not like they have to share similar interests or talk or anything.

"Q"-uotes

"I'm an outcast of the outcasts."—Stanford
"When did single translate into being gay?"—Miranda
"A pseudo-lesbian couple attend a right wing republican dinner party."—Carrie

---

Episode Four: "Valley of the Twenty-Something Guys"

Q-tastic Moment

Carrie labels the guys she sees at the bar: groovy guy, corporate guy, jock guy, underage guy, really good kisser guy. Admit it: that's what we all do when we're in a bar. We scan the crowd, and divide the men we see into

The Men

Character	Actor	Slept with	Notes	You might know him from such gay-friendly films and shows as
Brian	Josh Stamberg	Charlotte	Known as the "up the butt guy" for his love of anal sex	Six Feet Under
Skipper	Ben Weber			
Jon	Kohl Sudduth	Samantha	Twenty-something chef Samantha dates	54
Sam	Timothy Olyphant	Carrie	Twenty-something friend of twenty-something chef	Broken Hearts Club, First Wives Club

clear and distinct categories, whether it's by what they're wearing, how they're dancing, or how much you'd have to drink to sleep with them. At best, it's a way to cull the herd, and at worst, it's a fun way to pass the time.

"Q"-uote

"Front, back, whatever. A hole is a hole."—Samantha

Episode Five: "The Power of Female Sex"

Q-tastic Moment
Carrie sets off to test the theory that shopping can release the creativity of the unconscious. We've known

The Men

Character	Actor	Slept with	Notes	You might know him from such gay-friendly films and shows as
Neville	Charles Keating		An artist whose paintings of vaginas are on display in Charlotte's gallery, he asks if she would allow him to paint a portrait of her, well, you know.	Xena, Brideshead Revisited
Skipper	Ben Weber			
Gilles	Ed Fry	Carrie	French architect who leaves $1,000 for Carrie on the bedside table after a passionate night	

this to be the case for years. How else do you explain the benefits of devoting entire weekends to antiquing? Charlotte is asked by an artist from her gallery to sit for him. A theme is born!

Episode Six: "Secret Sex"

Q-tastic Trivia

First time Big and Carrie have sex. They're exhausted by the end. We are, too.

Charlotte admits to sleeping with an Orthodox Jewish artist, a clear and early indication that Charlotte's into Jewish guys!

The Men

Character	Actor	Slept with	Notes	*You might know him from such gay-friendly films and shows as*
Ted	David Aaron Baker	Miranda	Likes spanking videos	*The Music Man, Kissing Jessica Stein*
Mike	Michael Port		Carrie's straight friend with a secret girlfriend	
Shmuel	Glen Fleshler	Charlotte	Hasidic folk artist who Charlotte visits	

Episode Seven: "The Monogomists"

Q-tastic Trivia

Justin Theroux will show up again, as a different character later. Who? Keep reading!

Q-tastic Moment

When Carrie admits that she'd "... forsaken my girlfriends for my new boyfriend," we can all relate to dumping our friends, at least briefly, in favor of the new passion in our lives. Luckily, the true friends stick around, and we eventually come to the realization that though boyfriends may come and go, our friends are forever. A new guy enters our lives and, for the first few weeks, the sun rises and sets depending on his gym schedule. It's only when reality sets in, and we realize that he can't talk about anything other than how much he can bench do we realize we've been neglecting our friends and missing their conversation, counsel, and company. And we know it'll soon be our turn to wait until our friends remember that they've just forgotten about us.

"Q"-uotes

"Maybe you're on your knees, but you've got them by the balls."—Samantha

"My lover and I have a kind of '90s monogamy. We have

The Men

Character	Actor	Slept with	Notes	You might know him from such gay-friendly films and shows as
Michael	Jack Koening	Charlotte	Keeps pushing Charlotte's head down to his lap	*The Lion King on Broadway*
Rick	Michael Dale	Samantha	Realtor Samantha sees behind her other realtor's back	
Jared	Justin Theroux		Writer friend of Stanford Carrie meets after being disappointed with Big	*Strangers with Candy, Six Feet Under, Zoolander, Broken Hearts Club*
Skipper	Ben Weber	Miranda	Finally!	
Chunky Gay Guy	John Scurti		Interviewed about monogamy	*Rescue Me* episode entitled "Gay"

sex with other people, but we don't exchange fluids or phone numbers."—Chunky Gay Guy

"When life gets confusing, there's only one thing to do. Go to a fabulous party."—Carrie

Episode Eight: "Three's a Crowd"

Q-tastic Trivia

Big was married before. Huh? And we're just finding this out now? Amazing. In a ruse to meet the ex-wife, a children's book editor, Carrie sets up a meeting in which she pitches a story about a girl with magic cigarettes. The editor loves it, her bosses hate it. The world loses the next *Where the Wild Things Are*.

"Q"-uotes

"Threesomes are the blowjobs of the nineties."
   —Samantha
"If your friends won't go down on you, who will?"
   —Miranda
"Why is it that putting a tie around a man's neck is
   sometimes even sexier than taking it off?"—Carrie

The Men

Character	Actor	Slept with	Notes	*You might know him from such gay-friendly films and shows as*
Jack	Joseph Murphy	Charlotte	Really, really wants a three-way. Eventually convinces Charlotte, who literally gets pushed out of the way	*Rescue Me* episode entitled "Gay"
Ken	Jonathan Walker	Samantha	Married guy who decides to leave his wife for Samantha	

Episode Nine: "The Turtle and The Hare"

Q-tastic Moment

Stanford places a personal ad in an effort to meet a boyfriend. And though he does get a response, he's completely rejected when he meets the guy in person. And to make it worse? It's on a street corner. Poor Stanford! If only the Internet was as big a resource then as it is now. There's nothing worse than dating, except of course for

The Men

Character	Actor	Slept with	Notes	*You might know him from such gay-friendly films and shows as*
Jerry	Sebastian Roche			
Bernie Turtletaub	Tim Wheeler		Guy with notoriously bad breath who Samantha meets at a wedding. Her makeover of his outside can't change what he is inside—boring	
Personal Ad Guy	Merrill Holtzman		Dumps Stanford upon meeting him, on a street corner	

the date that doesn't happen. We're all worried that we'll be rejected, and can only hope that if it happens, it'll be done as painlessly as possible. Not in public. On a street corner. Within four seconds of meeting.

"Q"-uotes

"Even guys like me don't want guys like me."—Stanford
"I'd rather stay home with the rabbit than go out and deal with men."—Charlotte

---

Episode Ten: "The Baby Shower"

Q-tastic Trivia

Miranda has two sisters. They'll come up again later when Miranda's mother dies. Oh, did I just spoil that for you? Sorry. Miranda's mother lives a long and happy life. Better?

Carrie's address: 245 East 73rd Street. It doesn't really exist, so don't bother trying to find it.

Q-tastic Moment

Samantha throws herself an "I don't have a baby" shower to let everyone know she's fabulous. There's no rule that says we can't throw ourselves a party if we don't have a baby, or a house in the suburbs, or a husband to celebrate. And why shouldn't we all celebrate? So what if we're not about to give birth, when we just landed a great account at work, or repainted the living room, or

The Men

				You might know him from such gay-friendly films and shows as
Character	Actor	Slept with	Notes	
Jonathan	Blair Hickey		Guy who meets Charlotte at Samantha's party	

sat through a six-season marathon of our favorite television show. A party is in order!

"Q"-uotes

"All I have to do to meet the ideal man is give birth to him."—Miranda

"It's very strange when the life you never had flashes before your eyes."—Carrie

Episode Eleven: "The Drought"

Q-tastic Trivia

First time Big is in Carrie's apartment. It's not as big or grand as his, or even as Monica and Rachel's Greenwich Village manse, but we New Yorkers recognize its size, location, and rent-stabilization for the fantasy it is.

Carrie admits that she fears she'll pick up the *New York Times* one day and find that Big got married to someone perfect. Smells like foreshadowing to me.

"Q"-uotes

"There's a moment in every relationship when romance gives way to reality."—Carrie

"Men aren't that complicated. They're kind of like plants."
—Samantha

"If I make it to four months, I'm humping one of you."
—Miranda

The Men

Character	Actor	Slept with	Notes	You might know him from such gay-friendly films and shows as
Big				
Siddhartha	Anthony DeSando	.	Samantha's yoga instructor, who, despite his flirtations and tumescence, has taken a vow of Tantric celibacy	*Kiss Me, Guido*, *Party Girl*
Eddie	Ed Vassallo	Samantha	Meets horny Samantha during class and responds positively to her question "Wanna fuck?"	
Kevin	David Lee Russek	Charlotte	Prozac's effect on his libido ends his relationship with Charlotte	*Six Feet Under*
Construction Worker	Dann Fink		Catcalls Miranda every time she goes to Blockbuster	

Episode Twelve: "Oh Come, All Ye Faithful"

Q-tastic Trivia

Samantha tells a man she loves him. That can't be good.
Not a holiday episode, despite title.
Big and Carrie's first real breakup. They're exhausted. So
  are we.

The Men

Character	Actor	Slept with	Notes	You might know him from such gay-friendly films and shows as
Tom	John Benjamin Hickey	Miranda	Must shower immediately after sex	*Infamous, Life With Judy Garland: Me and My Shadows, Love! Valour! Compassion!, Cabaret* on Broadway
James	Jaime Goodwin	Samantha	He's great, but his small penis is killing Samantha, and not in the good way	
Allanne	Duane Boutte		Stanford's new boyfriend!	*Brother to Brother*

Q-gasmic Guest Star

Big's mother is played by Broadway diva Marian Seldes!

"Q"-uotes

"What is it about God and fashion that go so well together?"—Carrie

"Stanford and Allanne worship the same god: style." —Carrie

"Why, why, why does he have to have a small dick? I really liked him."—Samantha

"I love a big dick. I love it inside of me. I love looking at it. I love everything about it."—Samantha

CHAPTER THREE

Profile: Sarah Jessica Parker

Q
QUOTE

We couldn't help but wonder . . .
who could ever "Carrie" the show?

SOME OF the best shows, or at least those shows the Q community holds dear to its heart, feature four main characters. Think about it: *The Golden Girls*, *Designing Women*, *Will & Grace*, and to some degree, movies like *The Wizard of Oz* and *Dreamgirls*. All showcase four characters, each representing a different point on a compass, and therefore a different viewpoint. The four balance each other, allowing for differing, often hilariously different perspectives, and sometimes conflicts, which ultimately bring about the final resolution. But there's always one character just slightly more easy to relate to than the others. One is always just a little more open to possibilities, a little more of a blank slate, a little more like us. We had Dorothy Zbornack's no-nonsense attitude, Mary Jo Shively's struggling-to-get-by work ethic, and even Will Truman's implacable, but some-times over-the-top fastidiousness to project our own selves upon. And in *Sex and the City*, it's pretty clear that it's Carrie to whom we relate the most. Undeniably the linchpin of the crew, it is Carrie who is the most down-to-earth with her inquisitiveness, willingness to see different perspectives, and her every-woman strug-gles. She's the sun around which the other planets, each with its own marked characteristics, revolve. I think it's safe to say that if we couldn't relate to Carrie, the show would have been a failure, and it's safer still to say that the only person who could have played her, was, and is, Sarah Jessica Parker.

It's shocking to think that a native of Ohio could ever be seen as the embodiment of everything that is New York, but Sarah Jessica Parker, or "SJP" as we like to call her, now seems the most logical, natural, and lovely personification of The City imaginable. It was New York which first embraced the 14-year-old in 1979 when she starred in the title role of *Annie* on Broadway. And it was New York and the Broadway audiences who continued to herald her musical talent and undeniable charm through the years when she replaced Megan Mullally to star opposite her husband, and co-New York darling, Matthew Broderick, in the successful revival of *How to Succeed in Business Without Really Trying*. She later claimed the character of Princess Winifred in *Once Upon a Mattress*, putting her own stamp on this char-acter which had been originally played, and owned, by none other than Carol Burnett.

During her long career in Hollywood, spanning such wide and varied Q-loved films as *Footloose*, *Girls Just Want to Have Fun*, *LA Story*, *Hocus Pocus*, *Mars Attacks!*, *The Substance of Fire*, and *The First Wives Club*, as well as such television shows and specials as *Square Pegs*, *The Ryan White Story*, *The Sunshine Boys*, SJP brought her unconventional beauty, enormous talent, and wide and varied fan base to each of her roles. But it's her role as our favorite *New York Star* columnist that cemented her standing in American popular culture. Though each of the four actresses holds a special place in our hearts, SJP was able to bring a certain unique combination of strength, vulnerability, and openness to the part. We had to believe that she would make mistakes, get dumped, get swept off her feet, and be the girlfriend we all wanted, or wanted to be. She had to convey that she could be hopeful yet jaded, questioning yet sure of herself, damaged yet willing to heal, and beautiful on the inside and out. SJP worked as Carrie-as-us because it's easy for us to believe that SJP *is* us.

After the show, SJP was able to parlay her Hollywood clout into leading roles in films such as *Failure to Launch* and *The Family Stone*, but it was her ability to transcend her role as Carrie Bradshaw that allowed her to become, as she was labeled on Bravo's *Project Runway* during a guest spot, a "fashion icon." After being a spokesperson for Garnier Nutrisse hair coloring and posing in a short-lived stint for Gap, she went on to launch two fragrances of her own, Lovely and Covet. And to further her belief that "fashion isn't a luxury, and quality shouldn't be a privilege," she went on to create Bitten, her own low-price-high-quality fashion line, for Steve & Barry's.

Though for those for whom certain luxury items are a necessity, Manolo Blahnik did create a design, inspired by SJP, called, appropriately enough, the SJP.

Chris March, a contestant on *Project Runway* admitted, after practically weeping when he found out that SJP would be guest-judging designs for the episode, that he had moved to New York because of her and *Sex and the City*.

SEX AND THE SIDEBAR

When we were single, my roommates and I were glad to be able to navigate the choppy waters of dating in New York together. Many were the nights that one of us would arrive home, after a disastrous date, to find the other watching a rerun of *Sex and the City*. Carrie's on-again, off-again affair with Big; Miranda and Steve's opposing schedules; Charlotte's yearning for the perfect marriage; and Samantha's sexual exploits—we didn't have the same wardrobes or apartments, but these women were living our lives! In an effort to cheer me up after a particularly rough time with a man, my roommate even threw me a little *Sex and the City*-themed party, complete with pink champagne and a boxed set of DVDs. It helped to know that none of us were alone. We had each other, and we had Carrie!

—EK, New York, Massage Therapist and Gay Wedding Officiant

SJP's life and work have made her one of today's major and unquestionably popular gay icons. As Judy and Barbra before her, she's been able to consistently bring her non-traditional beauty and enviable talent to quality works of comedy and drama, as well as to meaningful businesses and charitable ventures. She shows that New York women can, in fact, have it all, with her down-to-earth attitude (including her insistence that her child attend public school), her stable and healthy family life and marriage, her business acumen, and her fashion-forward attitude. Deeply committed to charity work, including charities near-and-dear to the gay community, SJP takes her place among the great ladies of New York.

CHAPTER FOUR

The Cosmo

> We couldn't help but wonder . . .
> What's pink and wet after a long, hard day?

PEOPLE ALWAYS say that you'll never forget your first time. And they're right. When made properly, your first Cosmopolitan will change your world forever. Gaining national prominence as one of Carrie, Samantha, Miranda, and Charlotte's favorite drinks, there isn't a bartender anywhere in the country who doesn't serve a few of these a night. Sophisticated, classy, and refined, it's sweet enough for lightweights and strong enough for those who like a little kick. It's a drink that's become a statement about the drinker. If a woman orders one, it's a pretty sure bet that they're either from New York, or that they've watched *Sex and the City*. If a man orders a Cosmo, it's a pretty sure bet that he's gay.

Lots of cities may claim to be the birthplace of the Cosmo, especially South Beach, Florida, where bartender

Cheryl Cook is credited with creating a martini-glassed drink that was more visually appealing than a traditional martini. And though it's hard to determine where or when it originated, one thing's for sure: a Cosmo wouldn't be a Cosmo were it not for Carrie and the gang. And another thing's for sure: there's nothing else quite like it. The chilled glass, the twist of lime, the feel of the stem between your fingers as you hold it aloft to toast the start of the weekend, a Cosmo is more than a drink. It's a state of mind.

As a service to the community, we are pleased to present to you, for informational purposes only, the official International Bartenders Association recipe, as well as some variations to try for yourself, your partner, your mom, or whoever would enjoy a little taste of heaven.

International Bartenders Association

This one is a good, basic version. Just make sure you measure your measures, or you'll be under the table before the second round.

$2\frac{2}{3}$ measure citron-flavored vodka
1 measure Cointreau
1 measure fresh lime juice
2 measures cranberry juice
Add all ingredients into a cocktail shaker filled with ice.
  Shake well and strain into a large cocktail glass.
  Garnish with lemon slice.

From drinksmixer.com

Another simple, easy-to-make version. I appreciate that they took the time to tell us to shake "vigorously."

1 oz vodka
½ oz triple sec
½ oz Rose's® lime juice
½ oz cranberry juice

Shake vodka, triple sec, lime, and cranberry juice vigorously in a shaker with ice. Strain into a martini glass, garnish with a lime wedge on the rim, and serve.

From absolutdrinks.com

You might want to try this one after dinner in place of a dessert, or with Stoli Vanil, for a vanilla kick. It's my favorite.

4 parts Absolut Citron
12 parts cranberry juice
2 parts orange liqueur
1 dash lime juice

Chill a cocktail glass with ice or in the freezer. Pour Absolut Citron, cranberry juice, and orange liqueur into a shaker. Fill the shaker with ice cubes and shake it until the shaker is very cold. Empty the cocktail glass of ice and water. Strain the drink into the cocktail glass. Garnish with a lime (wedge).

From Stoli.com

Lots of cranberry flavors throughout, this one's a great Thanksgiving treat.

2 parts Stoli Cranberi
½ part triple sec
¼ part fresh lime juice
½ part cranberry juice
1 tsp cranberry jelly

Fill a shaker ⅔ full of clean ice. Add all the ingredients and shake hard. Strain through a fine sieve into a very tall martini glass. Garnish with a twist of lime.

From recipezaar.com

Pomegranate Cosmopolitan
A bit more exotic than the others, the pomegranate really does add a different and unexpected dimension!

1 cup vodka
¾ cup pomegranate juice
½ cup Cointreau or triple sec
½ cup lime juice
limes, twist for garnish
pomegranate seeds, for garnish

Combine vodka, pomegranate juice, Cointreau, and lime juice in a container. In small batches, shake mixture with ice in a cocktail shaker, then strain into chilled cocktail glasses. Garnish with a lime twist and a few fresh pomegranate seeds if desired.

White Cosmopolitan

This recipe will let you get a little sloppy without the worry of staining your white silk blouse.

5 ounces white cranberry juice
2 ounces citrus-infused vodka
½ ounce sweetened lime juice
ice cubes
limes, twist for garnish
4 cranberries, skewered onto a toothpick

Combine all ingredients, except garnish and cranberry toothpick, in a cocktail shaker with ice. Pour into a martini glass; garnish with lime twist and cranberry skewer.

Thai Cosmopolitan

An Asian-inspired spicy version. Not for those with wimpy taste buds, and probably best when not paired with equally spicy food.

Crystallized ginger
1½ ounces citrus-infused vodka
1½ ounces chili-infused vodka
1½ ounces cranberry juice

½ ounce pineapple-flavored liqueur
ice
pineapple wedge

Dip the rim of a martini glass in water and then rub in a plate of crystallized ginger to coat the rim. Pour vodkas, juice, and liqueur into a cocktail shaker with ice. Shake and strain into the glass and garnish with a pineapple wedge.

Cosmopolitan Slushy

Perfect for sitting around the pool on a hot summer's day, this version will bring you back to your childhood, while reminding you to bless the day you turned 21.

10 ounces citrus-infused vodka
½ cup Rose's® lime juice
2 cups cranberry juice
4 ice cubes, trays

Combine the vodka, lime juice, and cranberry juice in a pitcher with two cups water and stir to blend. Divide between ice cube trays and freeze at least four hours or overnight (the drink cubes will freeze only partially). Just before serving, empty trays into a large bowl and using a fork, break up cubes to loosen ice crystals (the ice will be slushlike). Spoon slush into a tall, stemmed glass and serve immediately.

Christmas Cosmopolitan

Screw the cookies, serve up a batch of these and you and Santa will be able to survive the holidays in style.

1½ ounces rosemary-flavored vodka
½ ounce triple sec or Cointreau
1 ounce cranberry juice
1 inch rosemary sprigs for garnish
cranberries for garnish

To make the rosemary-infused vodka, soak one coarsely chopped bunch of rosemary in a fifth of vodka overnight, then strain out the rosemary.

To make the drink: shake all the liquids together in a shaker, then strain into a martini glass. Garnish with one cranberry and one sprig of rosemary.

From Emeril: Emeril's New York City Cosmopolitan

Emeril gives us all a case of the BAM with this recipe, gloriously incorporating New York into the title and instructing us to serve immediately. Why wait?!

4 ounces citron-flavored vodka
2 ounces cranberry juice
½ ounce orange liqueur
1½ teaspoons fresh lime juice
2 thin twists lime, for garnish

SEX AND THE SIDEBAR

Like many young homos, I came to New York with big dreams of a fabulous lifestyle far grander than any my distant home-state afforded. And, like many young homos, I ended up as a waiter. I made three fantastic, absurd friends during my first few weeks at the restaurant. We were a formidable foursome, whether at the restaurant or after work.

True to all four-person groups in human history, we had a roaring slut, a big-hearted dim bulb, a high-strung smartass (yours truly), and our informal leader, the worldly wise cynic.

After our Sunday night shift, we would shove our way into our favorite gay bar, the now-closed "Works" on Columbus Avenue, to watch that week's episode. At some point, after way too many Cosmos, we realized that we four were that same classic quartet, just without the shoes and with half the money.

That realization cemented the bond of our friendship. No matter how far-flung we are around the country, or how long it's been since we were all on the town and fabulous together, we know that as soon as we sit down at a table, any table, it becomes *that* coffee shop table. And around that table, every conversation is the kind you could only have with your best friends on earth. It's a good feeling. Now all I need is the bartender, the baby, and the brownstone.

—JJ, New York, Editor
and Glue-Gun Marksman

Combine the vodka, cranberry juice, orange liqueur, and lime juice with ice in a cocktail shaker. Shake to combine and chill. Pour into two glasses filled with ice, and garnish each with one twist of lime. Serve immediately.

CHAPTER FIVE

Season Two

Episode One: "Take Me Out to the Ballgame"

"Q"-otes

"I don't think I'm ok, I just cried in your mouth."
   —Carrie

"Don't make me laugh. It's tragic."—Samantha

"I'm not drunk. I'm sedated for my pain."—Carrie

"Destroy all pictures where he looks sexy and you look happy."—Carrie

"I heard Nick Nolte had a ball lift."—Samantha

The Men

Character	Actor	Slept with	Notes	*You might know him from such gay-friendly films and shows as*
James	Jamie Goodwin	Samantha	Note change in spelling of his first name in end credits!	
Yankee Joe	Mark Devine		New to the team. Outside the locker room, Carrie tipsily asks him out.	*Six Feet Under*
Paul	Rob Bogue		Charlotte has to dump him because he keeps adjusting himself in public	*Oz*, an episode of *Whoopi* "No Sex in the City," and a series called *Sins of the City* *Dirty Dancing*

Episode Two: "The Awful Truth"

"Q"-otes

"Sex is not a time to chat."—Miranda
"He's a dog, not an oracle."—Charlotte
"What can I say? I need a big dick."—Samantha
"Personally, I don't like anything in my ass."—Stanford

Q-gasmic Guest Star

Bionic Woman's Molly Price as Susan Sharon. Charlotte adopts a dog to replace a relationship she's missing. In

The Men

Character	Actor	Slept with	Notes	You might know him from such gay-friendly films and shows as
Richard	Neal Jones		Carrie's friend's abusive husband	
Aaron	Neil Pepe	Miranda	Though a lover of dirty talk, it's too much for him when Miranda says she'll stick a finger up his ass	

this case, it's a dog named James, meant to take the place of a man. In the future, it will be a dog named Elizabeth Taylor Goldenblatt, to take the place of a baby.

Episode Three: "The Freak Show"

Q-tastic Trivia

Miranda's grandfather lives in Connecticut. So he's there, the rest of her family is in Pennsylvania. Any bets she went to one of the Seven Sisters schools?

Charlotte went to Camp Minnehaha in Maine. Well, it's not like we expected her to go to the B'nai Brith day camp every summer.

The Men

Character	Actor	Slept with	Notes	*You might know him from such gay-friendly films and shows as*
Harrison	Marc Kudisch		Has an S&M closet in his bedroom	*Bye Bye Birdie* Broadway musicals, including *Joseph, Beauty and the Beast, The Scarlet Pimpernel, High Society, The Wild Party, Bells are Ringing, Thoroughly Modern Millie, Assassins, Chitty Chitty Bang Bang*, and *The Apple Tree*
Ben	Ian Kahn	Carrie	Editor with Tweety tattoo. Carrie drives him off when he discovers her trying to break into a box she found in his closet	*CBS Schoolbreak Special: My Summer as a Girl* with Zach Braff

"Q"-otes

"If the world's fattest twins can find love, there's hope for us."—Carrie

"Are all men freaks?"—Carrie

"There is no world outside Manhattan."—Luke

"You can tell everything about a person by who their friends are."—Miranda

Character	Actor	Slept with	Notes	You might know him from such gay-friendly films and shows as
Mitch	Charlie Schroeder	Charlotte	Known as Mr. Pussy, he's re-nowned for his oral sex techniques, though eventually Charlotte realizes that's not enough to build a relation-ship on	*Strange Fruit*
PJ	Grant Varjas		Carrie's blind date	*The Laramie Project, Paradise Framed*
Bachelor #2	James Joseph O'Neil		Carrie's date who freaks out on theater line	
Max	Thomas Pescod		Carrie's blind date who shoplifts	
Luke	David Wike		Ben's friend who hasn't left Man-hattan in 10 years	

Episode Four: "They Shoot Single People, Don't They?"

"Q"-uote

"Orgasms don't send you Valentine's Day cards and they don't hold your hand in a sad movie."—Charlotte

The Men

Character	Actor	Slept with	Notes	*You might know him from such gay-friendly films and shows as*
Nevin	James Lecesne		Stanford's bf, works for *New York* magazine	*Gods and Monsters, Will & Grace, Further Tales of the City, Boys Life 2, Trevor*
Pakistani Busboy	Ajay Mehta		Comforts Samantha after she's stood up by William	
Josh	Mark Feuerstein	Miranda	Ophthalmologist Miranda has sex with to make up for faking it with him in the past	*In Her Shoes*
William	Robert Montano		A club owner who almost immediately starts using "we" to refer to himself and Samantha	*The Producers, Chicago,* Broadway: *On the Town, Kiss of the Spider Woman, Cats*
Tom	Tom Gilroy	Charlotte	Actor/handyman friend of Charlotte, who she sleeps with when he decides to move away	*Wild Tigers I Have Known, Everyday People, Post Cards from America*
Jake	Bradley Cooper		After hours club guy who flirts with Carrie	*He's Just Not That into You: The Movie*

Episode Five: "Four Women and a Funeral"

Q-tastic Trivia

Miranda buys an apartment. We renters are seething

The Men

Character	Actor	Slept with	Notes	*You might know him from such gay-friendly films and shows as*
Big				
Richard "Call me Dick"	Michael DeVries		Married philan thropist whose wife gets Samantha barred from every social event and restaurant in New York	Broadway: *Wicked, Hello, Dolly!, The Secret Garden, Grand Hotel, Cats*
Ned	Kurt Deutsch	Charlotte	Widower who collects women with his tale of woe	Founded Sh-k-Boom records, known for Broadway-inspired and cabaret artists
Leo DiCaprio			Meets Samantha on a volunteer project, gets her back in society's good graces and back on the lists for reservations	

with envy even as we try to figure out if her real estate agent can get us a deal.

Miranda's parents live in Pennsylvania. Any takers on the Seven Sisters bet?

Carrie and Big get back together. We took a nap so we aren't as exhausted. Let's go for another round.

While it seems that Leo DiCaprio appears in this episode, it's really just a silhouette of an actor playing him.

"Q"-otes

"You know what my version of hell is? Wearing rented, two-tone shoes."—Big

"Javier loved clothes. Unfortunately, he loved heroin more."—Carrie

"Don't fuck my husband, you hat-loving bitch."
    —Miranda

"I was watching Hard Copy and I kept thinking when they found me I would forever be the dead girl who watched bad TV!"—Miranda

---

Episode Six: "The Cheating Curve"

Q-tastic Moment

Charlotte exhibits the work of Yael, a lesbian painter from Brooklyn Heights, and is immediately drawn into the Yael's women-only world. We've all heard about the gay mafia. Many of us pay our annual membership dues and subscribe to the newsletters, but when it's actually seen in action, it just seems to right the world. So many social

The Men

Character	Actor	Slept with	Notes	You might know him from such gay-friendly films and shows as
Gareth	Sean Haberle		Toxic bachelor who cheats on Charlotte at gallery	
Ethan	Rob Campbell	Miranda	Watches porn while having sex	*Hedwig & The Angry Inch, Boys Don't Cry*
Thor	Chris John	Samantha	Personal trainer who shaves Samantha's pubic hair into a thunderbolt	*I Think I Do*

and institutional constructs seem to be so clearly designed to exclude us that when we see one of ours in action, it's a breath of fresh air. Only the most fabulous straights will ever get a glimpse into our secret societies (rules and requirements vary by state).

"Q"-otes

"I was a major lesbian in the fourth grade."—Miranda

"You can't expect to move to Wonder Woman's island and not go native."—Samantha

"The Power Lesbian. They seem to have everything. Great shoes, killer eyewear, and the secrets to invisible makeup."—Carrie

"It's a very neglected area, but people are starting to pay

attention . . . There's an entire business these days devoted to the upkeep and management of pubic hair. It says as much about you as your shoes."—Samantha

---

Episode Seven: "The Chicken Dance"

"Q"-otes

"I could have hired a nice gay decorator and none of this would have happened."—Miranda

"This is New York. Nothing is shocking. We've embraced public urination."—Big

The Men

Character	Actor	Slept with	Notes	You might know him from such gay-friendly films and shows as
Jeremy	Stephen Barker Turner		Miranda's friend who marries her decorator	
Big				
Rerun	Buzz Boushan	Samantha	Samantha forgot she had sex with him	
Martin	Mike Dooly	Charlotte	Usher at a wedding who seems perfect until his father makes a pass at Charlotte	

Episode Eight: "The Man, The Myth, The Viagra"

Q-tasic Trivia

Big calls Carrie his girlfriend. And that's girlfriend, not girl period friend period.

Donald Trump appears as himself. He does that a lot.

Miranda meets Steve when Carrie stands her up for dinner with Big. Cute meet alert!

The Men

Character	Actor	Slept with	Notes	*You might know him from such gay-friendly films and shows as*
Big				
Allan	Bruce MacVittie		Married guy who takes Miranda to comedy club	*Oz, 54, Stonewall*
Ed	Bill McHugh		Samantha's 72-year-old sugar daddy	
Steve	David Eigenberg	Miranda	Bartender who talks to Miranda when Carrie cancels their dinner to spend time with Big	

"Q"-uotes

"Samantha, a Cosmopolitan, and Donald Trump. You just don't get more New York than that."—Carrie

"While Samantha had little belief in the idea of happily ever after, she had a very strong belief in the idea of a smart cocktail at the end of the workday."—Carrie

---

Episode Nine: "Old Dogs, New Dicks"

Q-tastic Trivia

Steve likes it in the morning. Of course, he's a guy, so it isn't like there'd ever be a time when he wouldn't like it.

Big spends the night at Carrie's for the first time. We've been spending nights there for years now. He better not hog the covers.

Q-tastic Moment

The girls go to drag bingo to unwind and have fun, where Samantha meets an ex of hers, now a drag queen who goes by the name "Samantha." Proof that even the most fun events may contain their share of drama. It's just the way we roll.

"Q"-uotes

"I don't need one that can make its own carrying case."—Charlotte

"Uncut men are the best. They try harder."—Samantha

The Men

Character	Actor	Slept with	Notes	You might know him from such gay-friendly films and shows as
Mike	Alex Draper	Charlotte	Restaurant critic who gets circumcised for Charlotte, then dumps her so he can test out his new gear on other women	
Brad/ Samantha	Doan Mackenzie or Hedda Lettuce		Hockey player turned drag queen named Samantha	

Episode Ten: "The Caste System"

Q-tastic Trivia

This episode is the first of four directed by Allison Anders of Indy cinema fame. Fans of IFC get their props.

Carrie tells Big she loves him. Awww.

Big tells Carrie he fucking loves her. Awww.

Miranda sees Steve's apartment for the first time. She's a little grossed out. We're upset because it kind of looks like our place.

The Men

Character	Actor	Slept with	Notes	*You might know him from such gay-friendly films and shows as*
Harvey	James McCauley	Samantha	Rich man whose servant schemes to get Samantha dumped	
Wylie	Brian Van Holt	Charlotte	Young movie star who asks Charlotte to bring her scent back, on her hand, from the bathroom	
Jeremiah	Samuel Ball		Carrie's caterer friend, they meet at the party she attends with Big and he gets jealous	*Urbania*

"Q"-uote

"I'm not being a bitch, I'm just being myself."—Carrie

Episode Eleven: "Evolution"

Q-tastic Moment
The lines between gay and straight are blurred when nobody can quite figure out which side Charlotte's new

The Men

Character	Actor	Slept with	Notes	You might know him from such gay-friendly films and shows as
Stephan	Dan Futterman	Charlotte	Gay straight man who dates Charlotte	*Will & Grace* (Barry), *Urbania*, *The Birdcage*, writer/producer *Capote*
Dominic	John Shea	Samantha	The first man Samantha really loved, he returns, but dumps her before she can carry out her plan to dump him	
Joseph	Harry O'Reilly		Miranda's colleague, she finally agrees to go out with him, but can't get over his new, and bad, hair plugs	*Oz*

boyfriend plays on. Are there any distinctive behaviors of gay and straight men anymore? Does it matter?

"Q"-uotes

"This is a city where gay men are so out, they're in."
   —Carrie

"It's so not fair. All the good ones are straight. Even the gay ones."—Stanford

"The gay straight man was a new strain of heterosexual male spawned in Manhattan as the result of over-exposure to fashion, exotic cuisine, musical theater, and antique furniture."—Carrie

"A straight gay guy is just a guy who plays sports and won't fuck you."—Samantha

---

Episode 12: "La Douleur Exquise!"

Q-tastic Trivia

Big and Carrie break up. Again. Seriously, guys, we're exhausted. Well, maybe just one more.

Q-tastic Moments

Stanford goes to a downtown underwear club. Even if we haven't yet pushed the boundaries of our own comfort zones, many of us have wanted to, and we must admire Stanford for his courage. For the rest of us, how far are we willing to go, emotionally, especially given the poor body image lingering in the hearts and minds of so many gay men? We can all be inspired by Stanford's bravery to get out of the house, off the computer, and into his skivvies with a bunch of strangers—at least he's entering the real world where real people exist. And who knows, like Stanford, maybe we'll meet someone who likes us for what we are: a real person and not some sort of unrealistic standard.

Option for Carrie: living in Paris. Mon dieu!

"Q"-uotes

"Who am I to judge anyone? I had bangs in the 80s."
    —Carrie

"I haven't had good sex since before *Cats* was on Broad-
    way."—Stanford

The Men

Character	Actor	Slept with	Notes	You might know him from such gay-friendly films and shows as
Big				
Buster	James Urbaniak		Charlotte's shoe salesman with a foot fetish who gives her shoes for free or at major discounts	
Jack	Will Arnett	Miranda	Only likes doing it in public; his parents walk in on them	*30 Rock*
Gorgeous Young Hunk	Chris Payne Gilbert	In-shape guy who approaches not-so-toned Stanford at underwear club	*Broken Hearts Club*, and Season 4, episode 14!	

Episode Thirteen: "Games People Play"

Q-gasmic guest star

Jon Bon Jovi! Proof that the '80s produced many good things.

The Men

Character	Actor	Slept with	Notes	*You might know him from such gay-friendly films and shows as*
Guy in window	George Hahn		Hot guy across the way from Miranda's window. Though she thinks he's stripping and flirting with her, it turns out he's actually interested in the guy on the floor below her	
Don	John Dossett	Samantha	Guy so into sports, he'll only have sex with Samantha if his teams win	Broadway: *Gypsy*, Films: *Little Manhattan*, *Big Eden*, *Longtime Companion*
Seth	Jon Bon Jovi	Carrie	He makes bad relationship choices, and so does Carrie. They share a therapist and meet in her waiting room	

"Q"-uote

"It's the crazy ones that have the good pills."—Samantha

Episode Fourteen: "The Fuck Buddy"

Q-tastic Trivia

Skipper's back, this time with a girlfriend, though still pining for Miranda. Poor Skipper. We kind of forgot about him. He probably gets that a lot.

Charlotte asks a man out for the first time. We remember our first time. And by "remember" we mean one day we'll forget the pain and humiliation that followed immediately after.

"Q"-uote

"What I hate in life I love in sex."—Miranda

The Men

Character	Actor	Slept with	Notes	*You might know him from such gay-friendly films and shows as*
Kevin	David Lansbury	Miranda	Argumentative lawyer whose style in everyday life annoys Miranda, though she likes his aggressive nature in the bedroom	*Oz*, Angela's nephew!
John	Dean Winters	Carrie	Carrie's fuck buddy. Though they try for something more, they're totally incompatible outside the bedroom	*Oz*
Eric	Jon Patrick Walker		Charlotte asks two men out in one night. He's number one, who meets . . .	Off Bway: *Debbie Does Dallas*
George	Louis Aguirre		. . . number two during their date. They both never call again	hosted *Miss Florida Teen* and *Florida*

Episode Fifteen: "Shortcomings"

Q-tastic Trivia

Justin Theroux guest stars, again, this time as a completely different character. Told you he'd be back.
Charlotte's brother Wesley is divorcing his wife, Leslie.
   Wesley/Leslie becomes the Oprah/Uma of the coffee
   shop.

The Men

Character	Actor	Slept with	Notes	You might know him from such gay-friendly films and shows as
Roger	Daniel McDonald	Miranda	Divorced dad from gym whose son accidentally gets hit by Miranda	Broadway: *Steel Pier*
Vaughn	Justin Theroux	Carrie	A writer, Carrie loves his family a lot more than she loves him, and though he doesn't want to talk about his problem with very, very premature ejaculation, his mom does	
Wesley	Jack Mulcahy	Samantha	Charlotte's brother who is in the process of divorcing his wife, Leslie	

Vaughn's parents have my old couch in their living
room. I know this probably isn't particularly interesting to most people, but come on, how weird is that?

Q-tastic Moment

This episode serves as a meditation on what constitutes
family. Can we be family only to those with whom we
share blood? Hardly. As our community has proven,
time and again throughout the generations, families are
what you make them, and can be made of anyone you
wish. Your family is the group of people who accept you,
and love you for who you are, who support and encour-
age you, and who are with you through good and bad.
Vaughn's family doesn't think any less of Vaughn for being bad at relationships, nor do they care that his sister is
a lesbian. As long as she's not a Republican.

Q-gasmic Guest Star

Valerie Harper (*Rhoda*, Broadway: *The Tale of the Aller-
gist's Wife*) as Vaughn's mother, Wallis. Carrie loves her
more than she likes him. We all do.

"Q"-uotes

"When Franny told me she was a lesbian, I said great,
just as long as you're not a Republican."—Wallis

"The most important thing in life is your family. There
are days you love them and others you don't, but in
the end, they're the people you always come home to.
Sometimes it's the family you're born into and sometimes it's the one you make for yourself."—Carrie

Episode Sixteen: "Was It Good for You?"

Q-tastic Moments

Couple David and David, Samantha's gay friends, decide that it's time they tried having sex with a woman, and they ask Samantha to join them in bed. Unfortunately for her, though they get off to a good start, both Davids decide to opt out of exploring her, and suggest going out for gelato. So many of us have never been intimate with a member of the opposite sex. For some, it's just never been interesting, while others find it just plain icky. Samantha's sexual freedom gives us all the courage not only to experiment, but also to admit what we like, how far we can go, and what's, well, just too icky.

Miranda confesses to dating a guy who was in Over-eaters Anonymous. The seeds of a Krispy Kreme donut glaze/bodily fluid analogy are born.

"Q"-uotes

"Soon everyone will be pansexual. It won't matter if you're gay or straight."—Samantha

"I once fell asleep when a guy was doing me. It was the ludes."—Samantha

"It's very pretty, but no."—Gay David

"Not having a dick would be the thing that you did to turn them off."—Miranda

The Men

Character	Actor	Slept with	Notes	You might know him from such gay-friendly films and shows as
Bram	Kevin Flynn	Charlotte	Falls asleep during sex with Charlotte, prompting her to think she's bad in bed	
David	Sean Martin Kingston		Half of a gay couple who wants Samantha to be the first woman he and his partner sleep with	*The Producers*
David	Brad Hurtado		The other half of the couple	
Patrick	Richard Joseph Paul	Carrie	Alcoholic composer who trades his addiction for booze for an addiction to Carrie; when she tries to back off, he goes back to drinking	*CBS Schoolbreak Special: What if I'm Gay?*

Episode Seventeen: "Twenty-something Girls vs. Thirty-something Women"

Q-tastic Trivia

We meet Natasha, Big's new girlfriend, for the first time. Tall, beautiful, and, most important, *young*, she's everything Carrie didn't want her to be. She's everything we didn't want her to be, too.

The Men

Character	Actor	Slept with	Notes	You might know him from such gay-friendly films and shows as
Greg	Anson Mount	Charlotte	20-something she meets on her way to the Hampton Jitney who gives her crabs	*In Her Shoes*
Bradley	Patrick Breen		Doctor who Carrie meets at a party on the beach	Kevin Hill played gay nanny on *Will & Grace*, *Oz*, *East of A*, *Party of Five*

"Q"-uotes

"OK. This is really fun. How long do we have to stay?"
   —Miranda
"What was the allure of the twenties? On one hand, there's great skin tone, the thrill of fresh experience, and the sense of a consequence-free life full of seemingly endless possibilities. While on the other, there are horrible apartments, sexually inexperienced men, and embarrassing errors in fashion judgment."
   —Carrie
"Good on paper, bad in bed."—Samantha

Episode Eighteen: "Ex and the City"

Q-tastic Trivia

Big and Natasha become engaged, after only five months. Carrie's confused and livid. We're just really pissed.

Steve and Miranda get back together. Again.

Sarah Jessica Parker becomes "executive consultant" on the show. Though we don't quite know what that is, we're proud of our SJP, and hope she's getting a cut of the money.

Q-tastic Moment

The girls sing "Memories" in public for Samantha, who has never seen *The Way We Were*. Why this musical tribute? It's a chick flick. Piano bars aside, the movie,

SEX AND THE SIDEBAR

Just over a year ago, after having just met my partner, we sat down to one of those online "Which girl from *Sex and the City* are you?" quizzes. It was hilarious fun! I found out that he was the wild, sexy Samantha that I thought I was. And instead of Samantha, I was a Charlotte! Since the quiz, I've made a point to own my inner Charlotte and, accordingly, have raised my bar to more of a Park Avenue standard. My partner travels a lot for business these days, and as sad as I am about that, it does afford me ample time to make my home and family picture perfect without him getting in the way.

—KK, Vancouver, British Columbia,
Licensing Executive and Disco Inferno

The Men

Character	Actor	Slept with	Notes	You might know him from such gay-friendly films and shows as
Mr. Cocky	John Enos	Samantha	Cocky in manner and size of member, he's too big, even for Samantha, who tries and tries	

song, and the songstress are iconic to our community. I mean what could be gayer than a triumphant, self-assured, and luminous Barbra sending Robert Redford off into a life of white-bread blandness?

"Q"-uotes

"What was I going to do? Stand around and chit chat about the weather? The man has been inside me for God's sake."—Miranda

"Cosmopolitan plus scotch equals friendship with your ex."—Carrie

"Your girl is lovely, Hubble."—Carrie

CHAPTER SIX

Profile: Kim Cattrall

Q
QUOTE

We couldn't help but wonder . . .
What woman had the right package to survive in a man's world?

THE ONE marked characteristic of Samantha Jones is that she has sex like a man. Actually, she does a lot of things like a man. Fine, she doesn't pee like a man or shave like a man, but she's a successful businesswoman with her own apartment, unafraid to take chances, confident in her decisions, and proud of her ability to bed any man at any time. Samantha says what she thinks, asks for what she wants, and usually comes out on top. Now, while this sort of behavior is usually seen as admirable in men, it's often thought of as bitchy or unappealing in a woman. Samantha doesn't care. And we're glad of it. Samantha needed to be portrayed by a woman with confidence enough to go balls-out sexually, intelligence enough to make it believable, and charm enough to soften the edges. She also had to be able to prove that underneath the tough exterior lies a heart of humor and warmth.

As one of the last members of the old-school Hollywood studio system, British-born, Canadian-raised Kim Cattrall signed a contract with famed director Otto Preminger at age 19, appearing in 1975's *Rosebud*. After a Universal buy-out of her contract, and years of guest starring on such television shows as *Charlie's Angels, Quincy, Colombo, The Incredible Hulk,* and *The Nancy Drew/Hardy Boys Mysteries,* Cattrall burst into the public consciousness as Miss Honeywell in 1982's *Porky's,* playing a teacher with a particularly strong sex appeal and unique coital-verbosity, then going on to star in the first of the *Police Academy* films. Following up with starring roles in such seminal cult and Q hits as *Big Trouble in Little China* and *Mannequin,* her popularity entered warp drive as a naughty Vulcan with fabulous Bettie Page bangs in *Star Trek VI: The Undiscovered Country.* Her stage work, including turns in Arthur Miller's *The View from the Bridge* and Chekhov's *Three Sisters* proved her acting chops and her commitment to New York theater.

Cattrall's beauty, strength, comic timing, and undeniable appeal made her perfect for the role of Samantha. But she originally turned the role down, only to accept it after Sarah Jessica Parker signed on.

As if *Sex and the City* wasn't enough to make her a gay-household name, Cattrall cemented her stature in the Q community by starring in *Crossroads,* with the one and only Britney Spears, and then, after the show ended, in Disney's *Ice Princess.* Train-wreck pop divas and ice skating? Heaven!

Let's face it, what other actress would put herself out there enough to write a book called *Sexual Intelligence*, while at the same time bravely playing a woman who owns her sexuality enough to live a life without compromise? Cattrall has raised some eyebrow's in America's heartland, but her ability to take traditionally masculine characteristics and feiminize them catapulted her into the favor of the gay community.

The character of Samantha even took on breast cancer with her usual humor and panache. Some contend that Samantha's diagnosis of breast cancer was a punishment for past "sins," but Cattrall has been adamant that that wasn't the case, and that as a real woman, Samantha would face any challenges—and overcome them.

Cattrall's openness regarding her character's sex life, as well as own experiences, has undoubtedly done more to help further the dream of women controlling their own sexuality in America than most people give her credit for. Cattrall's on and off screen personas has served her career and our community well.

CHAPTER SEVEN

The City

QUOTE

We couldn't help but
wonder . . .
What's the city with all the
sex?

YOU KNOW, when people say "The City," they're talking
about New York.

To get a taste of the heightened reality that is the
New York of the girls, you might want to try the *Sex
and the City* Hotspots tour, offered by On Location
Tours. According to their Web site, for a mere thirty-
nine dollars, you'll be whisked from the front of the
Plaza Hotel to spots throughout Manhattan made familiar by the show. Granted, this whisking is done by
bus and not by Big's limo, but you'll also be given the
opportunity to, among other things, sit on Carrie's
stoop, have a cupcake where Miranda and Carrie did,
stop at a bar, and pass the shoe store where Carrie
shopped. The tour isn't particularly recommended for

children due to adult language and themes, but they'll let the little ones come with you if you say it's OK.

Of course, you could save your money and keep reading here, because as fabulous as this book has been so far, we're also about to give you a smattering of the best places to strap on your Manolos, or your whatever else you may want to strap on, and have an absofuckinglutely fabulous time:

One thing to know about The City is that when real New Yorkers talk about The City, they are talking about Manhattan. Brooklyn, The Bronx, Queens, and Staten Island do, technically, make up four-fifths of the city, but The City itself is The City. And The City is, in turn, divided into many different neighborhoods, including the Upper East Side (old money), the Upper West Side (new money), Midtown (which can include The Theater District, Times Square, Hell's Kitchen, and Kip's Bay), The Lower East Side, Chelsea, The West Village, The East Village, SoHo (South of Houston—and pronounced *How-ston*, not *Hue-ston*), TriBeCa (Triangle Below Canal), The Financial District, Chinatown, Little Italy, and NoLiTa (North of Little Italy). And though many New Yorkers may not know exactly which streets border each of these neighborhoods, everyone knows which nabes are best for shopping, eating, drinking, or finding a closet-sized apartment for an extraordinary amount of money.

In light of the show, the most impotant thing to know about The City is that The City Carrie and the girls live in is—we hate to break it to you—a bit unrealistic. In reality, the chances of running into people you know are as strong, and the lines to get into the clubs are as long, but it's important to note that in the TV City, the streets are cleaner, the clothes are more affordable for those on a budget, the cabs are more plentiful, and the tourists aren't nearly as annoying during lunchtime.

A Q Tour of The City We've Learned to Love from the Show

Union Square Area

City Bakery (18th Street between 5th and 6th Avenues): where Carrie and Samantha run into Nina and have cookies. Great food, a little pricey. Go early for lunch as it tends to get a little crowded.

Blue Water Grill (13th Union Square West): where Charlotte's date beats up a man. Great but overpriced seafood, jazz downstairs in the evenings.

Old Town Bar and Restaurant (18th Street and Broadway): where Carrie and New Yankee go for a drink. Been there forever with wood everywhere. Literally, as it's paneled, and figuratively as it's very popular for after-work drinks for straight New Yorkers, especially ex-frat boys. If you're looking for a taste of old New York, this is the place, and though beer and drinks are strong and plentiful, don't expect to find the best Cosmo. In addition to the bar, you'll find a restaurant serving great burgers up a very steep and creaky flight of steps.

ABC Carpet & Home (19th Street and Broadway): where Charlotte and Bunny go bed shopping. If you think you can just spend twenty minutes looking for a lamp, well, what are you thinking? Certainly that won't happen here, with six dizzying floors (or is it seven? Or twenty?) of chandeliers, Indonesian coffee tables, and more mid-century modern than you could possibly fit into a New York apartment.

Paul Smith (16th Street and 5th Avenue): Steve buys his very very expensive suit here. You can buy one, too, if that investment scheme is working out for you.

Il Cantinori (10th Street and University Place): where Carrie's ill-fated birthday bash crashed. A reliable neighborhood place, its proximity to NYU can bring in the younger crowd.

Bowlmor Lanes (University Place and 13th Street): where Carrie and Big bowl. You didn't think bowling could be au courant, did you? Here, you'll get carded right before you take the elevator up to this hip bowling alley, one of the only bowling spots remaining in Manhattan.

SoHo

The SoHo House (13th Street and 9th Avenue): a private, members-only club. Is it irony that the floor with steam rooms is called the "Cowshed"? This is the hotel where Samantha fakes her way in to use the pool.

Chelsea

Nell's (14th Street between 7th and 8th Avenues): where the girls went for drag bingo. Closed since 2004, Nell's is now an exclusive club called Plumm. Don't expect to be let in the door easily; you'll be much better off visiting any of the other gajillion gay bars, clubs, and restaurants in New York's most gay-centric neighborhood.

Tekserve (23rd Street and 6th Avenue): where Carrie and Aidan take her crashed computer. Usually filled with Chelsea boys with broken machinery, the geek-chic of the repair staff should not be underestimated.

West Village

Magnolia Bakery (11th and Bleecker Streets): where Carrie and Miranda ate cupcakes. The lines are always long at this neighborhood mainstay, but the cupcakes are definitely worth the wait.

Two Boots (West 11th Street and 7th and Greenwich Avenues): where Miranda and Carrie go for some real food after their raw food dinner is a bust. Blending Italy with New Orleans (get it? Two boots!), this famed pizzeria specializing in spicy crust and innovative toppings has opened in various parts of The City.

Slate (West 21st Street between 5th and 6th Avenues): where the gang takes Steve to help him forget about his testicular cancer. Very gay-friendly and down to earth, this pool hall is a great place to meet for fun and drinks.

Ray's Pizza (various locations): where Miranda and Steve have a quick lunch. One of New York's best original pizza joints, it's often imitated but never quite duplicated.

The Pleasure Chest (Charles Street and 7th Avenue): where Charlotte meets The Rabbit. Known far and wide for its wide variety of vibrators, lube, condoms, books, greeting cards, videos, costumes, gifts, ball gags, and bachelorette party accessories, The Pleasure Chest and the more female-centric Babeland (Mercer and Grand Streets) are more than happy to call a vibrator a vibrator, unlike Sharper Image (various locations) which only sells "neck massagers."

Trapeze School (West and Desbrosses Streets): where Carrie takes lessons. White knuckles abound at this iconic site off the West Side Highway, but it's so close to Chelsea and the piers that you're sure to get an eyeful of shirtless men rollerblading, jogging, or just walking by, so be glad there's a net.

Midtown

The Monkey Bar (54th Street and Madison Avenue): where Carrie and Big meet Ray the jazz guy. Though Ray says he owns the bar, he doesn't. A 70-year-old restaurant and bar, once considered the pinnacle of swanky New York style, The Monkey Bar has just received a new redesign and Asian-inspired menu. Fabulous décor (yes, there are monkeys here and there), great drinks and not-too-prohibitive prices make this New York mainstay a viable option for out-of-towners looking for a bit of the high life.

La Perla (Madison Avenue and 67th Street): where Carrie and Samantha shop for lingerie. More sexy skivvies than you could shake your fruit of the looms at, this lingerie boutique has several outposts around the city.

Takashimaya (Fifth Avenue and 54th Street): where the girls test fragrances. High-end but accessible Asian-inspired department store. Definitely try their downstairs café for tea or a light lunch.

Asia De Cuba (Madison Avenue and 37th Street): where Carrie and the girls wait for Aleksandr. The famed New York outpost of this national favorite is still going as strong as their drinks.

New York Public Library (42nd Street and 5th Avenue): where Miranda advises two girls to not pine for men who may just not be into them. One of the biggest and most famous libraries in the world, this is the one with the two lions in front. Impress your friends with this: The names of the lions are Patience and Fortitude. Told you this book would make you look good at parties!

The Learning Annex (53rd Street and Lexington Avenue): where Carrie teaches a class on how to find men in The City. Though her first class is a complete failure, Carrie can now claim to have taught at the same venue as such venerable politicos and celebrities as Henry Kissinger, Bishop Desmond Tutu, Rudy Giuliani, Donald Trump, and P. Diddy.

Bryant Park (42nd Street and 6th Avenue): where Carrie becomes fashion road-kill, this park behind the main branch of the library is home to New York Fashion Week. The entire park is covered in a giant tent. Which is exactly what some of the models look like as they sashay down the runway.

Vera Wang (39th Street and 7th Avenue): where Charlotte buys her wedding gown. Now located at Madison Avenue and 76th Street, Vera's flagship store is the fantasyland good little brides and their gay best men escape to between episodes of *Bridezilla*.

Upper East Side
Payard Patisserie (74th Street and Lexington Avenue): where Miranda almost buys incredibly expensive pastry to stave off having sex. One of the finest French restaurants around, it has a dessert menu to die for. Tell

yourself you're going there just for the sorbet or one, and only one, cookie, but at the last minute change your order and get the milk chocolate hazelnut candy bar with salted caramel sauce or the dark bittersweet chocolate soufflé with pistachio ice cream. It will be worth the extra time on the treadmill.

Tiffany's (57th Street and 5th Avenue): where Charlotte and Trey buy her ring. Once Audrey Hepburn nibbled her breakfast while staring longingly in its windows. Tiffany's has become not only an iconic New York store, but a must-see for any classic film fan (read: gay boy). Though you will look, and probably feel, a little silly munching on your Egg McMuffin while your boyfriend takes your picture, there's no harm in wiping the grease from your hands, walking through the doors, and browsing around. Oh, and when it's raining, they give you plastic bags to put your wet umbrella in. Can you say "free souvenir"?!

Prada (Broadway and Prince Street): where Carrie tries to get Berger to buy a shirt. They'll try to get you to buy one, too. You can't.

Barneys (60th Street and Madison Avenue): where Carrie leaves a "blind" Charlotte to take a call from Aleksandr. Probably one of the gayest mainstream department stores in New York, Barney's windows are breathtaking, and usually directed by Simon Doonan. Take a look around at the incredible quality of the merchandise, the incredible quality of the gay staff, and then either head downtown to the Barneys Coop, or wait for the sample sales.

Tasti D-Lite (various locations): where Charlotte and Harry go for dessert. Nobody quite knows how these frozen delicacies are made, but that doesn't stop hordes of people from lining up night after night for a low-calorie treat.

Charlotte's apartment (77th Street and Park Avenue)

Carrie's apartment (73rd Street between Third and Second Avenues)

Upper West Side

Manolo Blahnik (54th Street and 6th Avenue): where Carrie buys her shoes. And we want to. If there was ever a master footwear designer, it's Blahnik. "Shoes," he writes on his Web site, "transform a woman." And if you don't agree, then put down this book, hand in your gay card, and go skipping in your two-for-one Payless espadrilles out of here.

Holy Trinity Church (82nd and Broadway): where Charlotte and Trey marry. Dating from 1900, this church is one of the finest examples of medieval architecture in New York.

Loews Sony Movie Theatre (Broadway and 68th Street): where Carrie and Berger have their first date. One of the first mega-Cineplex's in The City, it has stadium seating and is often the site of advance or special screenings.

The Fountain at Columbus Circle: where Carrie and Aidan break it off, despite looking fabulous. Located at the intersection of everything (well, not everything, just Broadway, Central Park West, and 59th Street), this is the location of the newly-built Time Warner Center. Home to a variety of high-end retailers, corporate offices, and Jazz At Lincoln Center, it also boasts the most expensive apartments in New York.

Lincoln Center: where Aleksandr dips Carrie into an

overwhelming vat of over-the-top romance, causing her to faint. Lincoln Center is home to, among other things, The Julliard School, The Metropolitan Opera, New York City Ballet, and The New York Public Library for the Performing Arts. In other words, you won't be able to swing your manbag without hitting a gay guy in tights or a tux. A cultural hub of The City, its fountain is so iconic as to have been featured in such movies as *Moonstruck* and *The Producers*.

Miranda's apartment (78th Street and Amsterdam Avenue)

Meatpacking District

Samantha's apartment (Gansevoort and Greenwich Streets). Once the home to scads of gay bars and sex clubs, the neighborhood has transformed itself into one of New York's most expensive, fashionable, and expensive areas. Meaning that the streets, once littered with tranny hookers, bears, leather queens, and straight businessmen who somehow got turned around and found themselves in a club sniffing each others underwear are now crawling with celebutants and Eurotrash. Pity, really.

Financial District

Staten Island Ferry (South Ferry Terminal): the girls take the ferry to go to Staten Island, and Charlotte claims she'll marry by the end of the year. Though you may not have the same luck on this boat, which serves as the main mode of conveyance to thousands of Staten Islanders who commute into Manhattan every day, you'll get one of the best views of The City. Hold on to your pearls for the best part: it's free!

New York Stock Exchange (Wall and Broad Streets): Carrie rings the opening bell when her newspaper goes public. If you're like Samantha, and get turned on by a bunch of sweaty men in suits trying to get it ("it" being stocks) up, then troll around this neighborhood after the closing bell rings. Filled with exhausted men who have either made or lost millions, you may be able to find someone willing to buy you drinks, or at least to let you help them drown their sorrows.

Helena Rubenstein Beauty Gallery (Spring and Wooster Streets): where Samantha couldn't get serviced properly. And now, neither can you. It closed.

And just because we have to admit that The City is indeed more than Manhattan:

The Bronx

Home of Yankee Stadium, where the girls go to blow off steam and peek into the locker room. Trying to shirk its reputation as crime ridden and dangerous, this borough's many green spaces, as well as world famous zoo and stadium, keep people coming back to visit. And to live there, too.

Brooklyn

Where Smith's play launches his career, and where Miranda and Steve move. Based on the proximity to the Brooklyn Bridge, the play was probably mounted somewhere in DUMBO (Down Underneath the Manhattan Bridge Overpass). Once a no man's land of warehouses and abandoned, well, everything, this area is quickly becoming the new It place to be. Condos, restaurants,

SEX AND THE SIDEBAR

After dating hordes of men after moving to The City a few years ago, I never cease to be amazed at how there seems to be an episode for just about every dating experience I've had. It's gotten so bad that the show's characters' names are the same as the "characters" in my life. Recently, I was watching a rerun of "Shortcomings" with my boyfriend, when, halfway through, I realized it was the one in which Samantha falls for the guy who is perfect in every way, except the one most important to her. As the girls sat around talking about him, I realized that not only did he have the same name as the boyfriend, who was sitting on the couch next to me, but he also suffered from the same . . . problem. "Change the channel." I coughed quickly as I scurried to grab his remote control (notably an oversized remote, as if in an attempt to compensate). "I've seen this one already."

As if that weren't enough, I related to Carrie in the episode "I Heart New York," when she considered The City her boyfriend. Yeah, it can be dirty and weird and even downright mean, but after a world filled with random and less-than-ideal men, at least *it* has the Chrysler Building. And even on nights when you don't necessarily feel like strapping on your stilettos and conquering the town, there's a certain deliciousness in watching the show from your very own cramped New York apartment, with The City's most attractive quality—possibility—lurking just outside your door. Suddenly, the fact that everything can change at any moment becomes a good thing. How many men can offer you that?

—LW, New York, Editrix and Club-hopper

and boutiques pop up every day. And though never named, Miranda and Steve probably move to Brooklyn Heights. Just across the East River from Manhattan, it's probably as far from The City as Miranda would want to go, but filled with brownstones and all types of people and families, including plenty of families with two mommies. It's a true Brooklyn neighborhood. Remember the Huxtables? They lived there. And so do I!

Staten Island

Where the girls went for the fireman contest. Yeah. Umm. . . . Staten Island. It's the most Republican borough of them all. They've got a mall. And the Verrazano-Narrows Bridge, the one that connects to Brooklyn, was once the longest suspension bridge in the world and featured in *Saturday Night Fever*. Can I stop now?

Queens

Borough where you'll find both major New York airports, Shea Stadium, The US Open, and the gateway to Long Island, the end of which is the Hamptons, where the girls spend a few summer days, getting crabs from young men they meet on the bus, running into their ex-boyfriends, throwing melons through windows, and watching a gay guy marry a woman. Let's go Mets!

In the real New York, we have to deal with the bothersome lack of proper lighting, no hairstylist working on us before we leave the house, and very little makeup. But it's still The City to us. Our City. The City where a million dreams are realized, some hearts are broken, but you're always, always, among friends.

CHAPTER EIGHT

Season Three

Episode One: "Where There's Smoke . . ."

Q-tastic Trivia

Sarah Jessica Parker becomes Producer. How cute, she's a producer, and Matthew Broderick was in *The Producers*. It's cute, right? Right?

"Q"-uotes

"I'd like to show him my lower Manhattan."—Samantha

"Staten Island was like a quaint European country. The American music was twenty years behind and you could smoke wherever you wanted."—Carrie

I like a firefighter with love handles. It gives you something to hold on to when you ride them down the side of a burning building."—Bill

"If she falls over I will never stop laughing."—Miranda

"Ladies, let me tell you about his cock . . ."—Samantha

"With no man in sight, I decided to rescue my ankles from a life of boredom by purchasing too many pairs of Jimmy Choo shoes."—Carrie

The Men

Character	Actor	Slept with	Notes	*You might know him from such gay-friendly films and shows as*
Arthur	Brad Beyer		Charlotte's white knightmare, he keeps punching people wherever they go	
Bill	John Slattery		Running for NYC Comptroller, he eventually lets it be known that he likes to get peed on	*Will & Grace* (Will's brother), *Desperate Housewives*
Ricky	Michael Lombardi	Samantha	Firefighter participating in the contest Carrie's judging, he's a fantasy that turns into harsh reality	

Episode Two: "Politically Erect"

Q-tastic Trivia

Steve wants to be exclusive. We're touched, and can't help but notice that someone's been working out a bit.

Steve tells Miranda he loves her. And we love him for it. Did you notice he's been working out?

Q-tastic moment

In order to spare Stanford's feelings, Carrie tells him the guy he likes at the party is straight—it's not that he's just not interested. We all rely on our friends to tell us the little white lies that do nothing more than keep the world spinning without devastating us.

"Q"-uotes

"I was adept at fashion. He was adept at politics. And really, what's the difference? They're both about recycling shopworn ideas and making them seem fresh and inspiring."—Carrie

"The country runs better with a good looking man in the White House. Look what happened to Nixon; no

The Men

Character	Actor	Slept with	Notes	You might know him from such gay-friendly films and shows as
Bill	John Slattery	Carrie	Carrie finds out he wants her to pee on him	Mad Men
Steve				
Jeff	Anthony Alessandro	Samantha	Short guy who wins Samantha over with his ability to make her laugh	
Greg	Donnie Keshawarz		Flirts with Charlotte at party, gets back with ex	Broadway: Tarzan

one wanted to fuck him, so he fucked everyone."
    —Samantha
"I don't believe in the Republican party or the Demo-
    cratic party. I just believe in parties."—Samantha
"Hello. I represent the queer vote."—Stanford

Episode Three: "Attack of the Five Foot Ten Woman"

Q-tastic Trivia

As Carrie feared, she finds out that Big has gotten
    married by reading about it in *The New York Times*.
    Why doesn't anyone pay attention to foreshadowing?
Magda (Lynn Cohen), Miranda's housekeeper, makes her
    first appearance. We appreciate, and try to emulate,
    her condom-organizing skills. Easier said than done.

Q-tastic Moment

Carrie feels badly about herself when comparing herself
to Natasha, and we relate. We're all comparing aspects
of ourselves to other people every day. Whether it's our
careers, our bank accounts, our clothes, or our bodies,
we're in a constant battle to triumph in the daily meta-
phorical pissing contests we construct for ourselves.

"Q"-uotes

"This is what I hate about the Sunday *Times*. This, and
    all the country houses I can't afford."—Miranda
"These bitches need to be put in their places."—Samantha

The Men

Character	Actor	Slept with	Notes	You might know him from such gay-friendly films and shows as
Kevin	Christopher Sieber	Massage therapist whose reputation for going down on clients is well-known, though he doesn't provide that service for Samantha		*It's All Relative* Broadway: *Spamalot, Into the Woods, Thoroughly Modern Millie, Triumph of Love, Chicago, Beauty and the Beast*

"What's in your goody drawer, *Robert's Rules of Order*?"—Miranda

"I didn't grow up in a naked house."—Charlotte

"Helena Rubenstein is a civilized place for civilized people."—Manager

"I paid good money expecting to be eaten out!" —Samantha

Episode Four: "Boy, Girl, Boy, Girl . . ."

Q-tastic Trivia

It's the second time one of Charlotte's artists asks her to model. We get it, she's pretty, but isn't there some sort of artist/gallery worker code of ethics or something?

Miranda and Steve tell one another they love each other and move in together. Finally! Seriously, Steve, keep up those workouts.

Q-tastic Moments

Charlotte's gallery has a drag king art show. Charlotte and the girls' ruminations on what's seen as masculine, feminine, and the slight differences or quick-and-easy changes that balance the scale from one side to the other are proof that we're all just people who, depending on the clothes we wear, or the way we're lit, can be seen many different ways.

As open as Carrie is to sexuality, she's got her limits, and after exploring the idea of bisexuality from a variety of different angles, the challenge of a relationship in which she'd always be wondering if she can be replaced by a man is too much for Carrie to bear.

Q-gasmic Guest Star

Alanis Morissette plays Carrie's new boyfriend's ex-boyfriend's partner's newly partnered ex-wife who kisses Carrie during a confused grown-up version of the childhood game of spin-the-bottle. We're all a little bi- by the end.

"Q"-uotes

"Women dressing like men is very popular right now."—Samantha

"When you're gay, everyone can wear everyone's underwear."—Stanford

"I don't believe it's officially a date without cocktails."
—Carrie

"I don't think you're allowed to be bisexual in Colorado."
—Miranda

"I'm trisexual. I'll try anything."—Samantha

"I'm very into labels. Gay. Straight. Pick a side and stay
there."—Charlotte

"I'm not even sure bisexuality exists. I think it's just a
layover on the way to Gaytown."—Carrie

"The bad news is, you're fired. The good new is, now I
can fuck you."—Samantha

"I was Alice in Confused Sexual Orientation Land."
—Carrie

The Men

Character	Actor	Slept with	Notes	*You might know him from such gay-friendly films and shows as*
Baird	Donovan Leitch	Charlotte	Drag king photographer, shoots Charlotte	
Sean	Eddie Cahill	Carrie	Bisexual twenty-something whose sexual history, and openness, is too much for Carrie	
Matt	Chris Tardio	Samantha	Samantha's new assistant. His phone and business manners leave a lot to be desired	

Episode Five: "No Ifs, ands, or Butts"

Q-tastic Trivia

We meet Aidan for the first time (and Pete, Aidan's dog, who humps Carrie's leg upon their first meeting), as Carrie and Stanford go furniture shopping. Cable home-renovation shows immediately cast hot carpenters.

Carrie quits, or at least tries to quit, smoking. We're glad, as the whole emphysema thing really takes away from the outfit.

Q-tastic Moment

Stanford meets Marty, described as "warm, stylish, and classic gay," who he really likes, but is put off by his extensive doll collection. Is there a bias about gayness within the community itself? Uh . . . yeah. Just take a look online to see the labels and descriptors people use for themselves, and what they're looking for in others. Would a "Daddy" date a "Theater Queen?" Would a "Straight-acting" investment banker bring his "Bear" boyfriend to the company holiday party? Maybe, maybe not, but by creating categories of gayness, and acceptability, we've achieved our own brand of the paper-bag test.

"Q"-uotes

"That wasn't Black talk, that was Sex talk."—Samantha

"The dog-humping aside, it was one of those perfect New York Saturday afternoons."—Carrie

"Stanford wondered if he was enough of a queen to make love to a queen who collected queens." —Carrie

"I just can't see myself getting all excited because my boyfriend's three-foot Lady Di doll is arriving from QVC."—Stanford

The Men

Character	Actor	Slept with	Notes	You might know him from such gay-friendly films and shows as
Aidan	John Corbett			
Marty	Donald Berman		His extensive doll collection turns Stanford off	
Brad	Ross Gibby		Charlotte's face-licking bad kisser	
Chivon	Asio Highsmith	Samantha	African-American music scout, his sister drives a wedge between him and Samantha	Zoolander

Episode Six: "Are We Sluts?"

Q-tastic Trivia

Miranda's number: Forty-two. We all try to do our own math.

Aidan and Carrie do it. We then try to figure out if we have to add one if we're the only one in the room.

Q-tastic Moment

Samantha moves to the once rundown, prostitute- and sex-club-infested but now ridiculously trendy and expensive neighborhood of the Meatpacking District. By leaving her uptown building, she shucks off her neighbors' uptown repression and embraces the vibe and energy of downtown.

"Q"-uotes

"How many men is too many men?"—Carrie

"I can't tonight. I have Chlamydia."—Miranda

"They practically chased me with torches like I'm Fuckenstein."—Samantha

The Men

Character	Actor	Slept with	Notes	*You might know him from such gay-friendly films and shows as*
Aidan	John Corbett	Carrie	Their first time	
2 A.M. Guest	Carl Evans	Samantha	Late-night guest of Samantha, he not only lets a thief into the building behind him, but also serves as the straw that breaks the camel's back and turns the building against her	
Alexander	Christopher Orr	Charlotte	Mild-mannered in every respect, he can't stop saying "you fucking bitch you fucking whore" during climax	

Episode Seven: "Drama Queens"

Q-tastic Trivia

We meet Trey as Charlotte flees her mock date and falls in front of a cab. There's nothing hotter than a guy who doesn't care that the meter's running.

- Steve's mother is mentioned for the first time; Miranda doesn't want to meet her. We kinda do. Miranda and Steve have sex in the laundry room. There must be something about the smell of Snuggle.

"Q"-uotes

"You should know I get a tad bitchy from time to time."—Carrie

"I'm living with Skidmark Guy."—Miranda

"When your boyfriend is so comfortable he can't be bothered to wipe his ass, that's the end of romance, right there."—Miranda

The Men

Character	Actor	Slept with	Notes	You might know him from such gay-friendly films and shows as
Mark	Billy Wirth	Samantha	Introduces Samantha to Viagra	
Dennis	Ethan Sandler		Charlotte's married friend, he sets up an imaginary date with a friend of his so he can make his move	Will & Grace

Episode Eight: "The Big Time"

Q-tastic Trivia

Carrie lost her virginity in eleventh grade to a boy
named Seth. Seriously? That guy?

Charlotte and Trey declare their love for each other. We
declare our love for their fairy tale beginnings. Wait,
don't fairy tales usually have a witch . . . ? Steve wants to
have a baby, Miranda doesn't. We pick up the diction-
ary to learn the definition of "irony." Trey credits his

The Men

Character	Actor	Slept with	Notes	*You might know him from such gay-friendly films and shows as*
Len	Robert Lupone	Samantha	Old neighbor of Samantha's, she sleeps with him when she thinks she's getting old and can't do any better	Broadway: *A Chorus Line, Angels in America* Patti's brother!
Late night guest		There when Chinese is delivered. Doesn't say anything, and is on screen for just a few seconds.		

mother, and her poor gift selection, for bringing Charlotte into his life. "Witch" reminds me . . .

"Q"-uotes

"My vagina waits for no man."—Samantha

Episode Nine: "Easy Come, Easy Go"

Q-tastic Trivia

Big wants to leave Natasha after only seven months. We
   wanted it earlier, but with all the paperwork . . .
Big tells Carrie he loves her. Now? Now he tells her? Men.
Charlotte sort of proposes to herself, Trey agrees with
   "alrighty." We're sort of confused.

Q-gasmic Guest Star

Frances Sternhagen (*Misery*, *Cheers*; Broadway: *Morning's
at Seven*, *Steel Magnolias* (stars as Bunny, Trey's mother)

"Q"-uotes

"There's always a contest with an ex. It's called "who'll
   die miserable?"—Samantha
"There should be some sort of city-funded breakup
   housing for those who find themselves in need . . .
   like a big orphanage filled with white beds where old
   boyfriends can think about what they did wrong and
   cry themselves to sleep in a clean, safe environ-
   ment."—Carrie

The Men

Character	Actor	Slept with	Notes	You might know him from such gay-friendly films and shows as
Adam	Bobby Cannavale	Samantha	Suffers from Funky Spunk	*Will & Grace, The Night Listener, Happy Endings, Oz,* Theater: Rudnick's *The Most Fabulous Story Ever Told,* Coward's *In Two Keys*

"He's older than water but never forgets a martini."
—Bunny

"Of course he just loves getting head. But then what man doesn't?"—Samantha

"We can analyze this for years and never know. I mean they still don't know who killed Kennedy."—Miranda

"You heard me. Your spunk is funky."—Samantha

"Easy? You men have no idea what we're dealing with down there. Teeth placement and jaw stress and suction and gag reflex and all the while bobbing up and down moaning and trying to breathe through our noses. Easy? Honey, they don't call it a job for nothing."—Samantha

Episode Ten: "All or Nothing"

Q-tastic Trivia

Charlotte's place settings cost over a thousand dollars at Bergdoff's. I hear there's a sale at Century 21, though.

The Men

Character	Actor	Slept with	Notes	You might know him from such gay-friendly films and shows as
George	Josh Hamilton	Miranda	Phone-sex colleague from Chicago, Miranda ends the relationship when she discovers he's having phone sex with other women	*Absolutely Fabulous, Urbania*

Aidan and Carrie declare their love for each other. Hey, the man's good with his hands.

Cough syrup and Fanta soda over ice is Samantha's mother's cure-all. My people prefer chicken soup and a good heaping of guilt for getting sick in the first place, but whatever works for you.

"Q"-uote

"I can smell the guy on your sheets. Wood chips and Paco Rabanne."—Big

Episode Eleven: "Running with Scissors"

Q-tastic Trivia

We meet Anthony, played by Mario Cantone. A stylist friend of Samantha's, he's hired to help Charlotte

organize her wedding. Remember him from
Steampipe Alley? God, that was funny. God, he
was gay.

The hotel on 56th and 8th is a good place to have an
afternoon tryst. Because you'll run into people at The
Plaza. Tell me about it.

The Men

Character	Actor	Slept with	Notes	You might know him from such gay-friendly films and shows as
Tom	Sam Robards	Samantha	Known as the "Male Samantha," he won't have sex with her, in his swing or elsewhere, until she gets an AIDS test	*Prêt-à-Porter*, *American Beauty*
Anthony	Mario Cantone		Stylist friend of Samantha who helps Charlotte with her wedding	*The View*, *Kathy Griffin*, Broadway: *Laugh Whore*, *The Violet Hour*
Sandwich Guy	Adrian Reider		Dressed in costume, will only say "bite me" to Miranda as she walks by. Though initially insulted, she's intrigued	

"Q"-uotes

"The only sex test she'd ever taken was the *Cosmo* quiz."—Carrie

"We're looking at wedding gowns. Could you not talk about AIDS right now?"—Charlotte

"You want pasta, you go to Little Italy. You want wedding, you go to Wang."—Anthony

---

Episode Twelve: "Don't Ask, Don't Tell"

Q-tastic Trivia

Charlotte gets married. We see her father, who doesn't speak, walk her down the aisle. Her brother Wesley is nowhere to be seen. Weird, no? Yes.

"Q"-uotes

"I can get the sails up, I just can't get it into the harbor."—Trey

"I like the idea of men in skirts. Easy access." —Samantha

"Could you please not use the F word in Vera Wang?" —Charlotte

"It's romantic until he can't figure out where to put it in."—Samantha

"The wedding was complete. Charlotte had something old, something new, something borrowed, and someone Samantha blew."—Carrie

The Men

Character	Actor	Slept with	Notes	You might know him from such gay-friendly films and shows as
Harris	Clark Gregg	Miranda	Miranda meets him at speed dating, telling him she's a stewardess. He says he's a doctor, but he's really a manager at Footlocker	*Will & Grace, A Woman Named Jackie*
Caleb	Ritchie Coster	Samantha	Trey's Scottish cousin, whose accent is incomprehensible	

Episode Thirteen: "Escape from New York"

Q-tastic Triva

Studio executives and Matthew think that transferring Carrie's column to the big screen would require fleshing out the central relationship. Will this happen in the movie?

Q-gasmic Guest Stars

Sarah Michelle Gellar (*Buffy the Vampire Slayer*) plays a junior development exec at a company that wants to option Carrie's column for a movie

Matthew McConaughey (*Dazed and Confused, Failure*

The Men

Character	Actor	Slept with	Notes	You might know him from such gay-friendly films and shows as
Garth	James MacDonald	Samantha	Dildo model who wants to read poetry to Samantha and move to New York with her	*Buffy*
Jason	Edward Kerr		Goes after prettier women in bar	
Matthew McConaughey	himself		Cad	

to Launch) appears as a cad version of himself. Though he (unfortunately) keeps his shirt on for the entire episode, he and Sarah Jessica Parker later go on to star together in *Failure to Launch*

"Q"-uotes

"It's LA. Nobody cares if your egg whites come with a side of cock."—Samantha

"My husband can't be impotent. He's gorgeous." —Charlotte

"Cars are to Los Angeles what handbags are to New York."—Carrie

Episode Fourteen: "Sex and Another City"

Q-gasmic Guest Star

Vince Vaughn (*Swingers, The Wedding Crashers, Old School*) as Keith, Carrie Fisher's house sitter who Carrie thinks is a Hollywood bigwig.

"Q"-uotes

"Samantha had worshipped Hugh Hefner ever since she was old enough to steal her father's *Playboy*s."
—Carrie

"In New York, a first date is dinner and a movie. In LA, it's lunch and seeing a $3.4 million house."
—Carrie

The Men

Character	Actor	Slept with	Notes	You might know him from such gay-friendly films and shows as
Lew	Sam Seder		Ex-Letterman writer friend of Miranda's who's gone LA	
Hugh Hefner	Himself		Samantha's hero	
Ian	Marty Rockham		A guest at the Playboy mansion, he offers to buy Charlotte boobs	

"Lew may be the perfect guy . . . he's an ideal combination of the two coasts. He's still a New Yorker at heart, but he's lost all his angry neurosis. And thirty pounds."—Miranda

---

Episode Fifteen: "Hot Child in the City"

Q-tastic Trivia

Charlotte would name her vagina Rebecca. We all immediately try to remember what we've named our special parts.

The ladies have lunch in the MTV cafeteria. I know this because I've been there. Saw Dave Holmes there once. Gay, you know.

Q-gasmic Guest Star

Anita Gillette (*Match Game*, *Love, American Style*, Broadway: *Gypsy*, *Cabaret*, *Brighton Beach Memoirs*) plays Mrs. Adams

"Q"-uotes

"[Wonder Woman!] With the bracelets and the tiara. I used to love that even her accessories had super powers."—Carrie

"Not sexy, Honey. Drop him immediately. Here—use my cell phone."—Samantha

"That was so *Afterschool Special* of you."—Miranda

The Men

Character	Actor	Slept with	Notes	*You might know him from such gay-friendly films and shows as*
Wade	Cane Peterson	Carrie	Comic book guy who lives with his parents	
Lance	James Villemaire		Editor who dates Miranda	*Isn't She Great?*
Dr. Talley	Ron McLarty		Trey and Charlotte's therapist	

"One client, rather whimsically, dubbed his anus the 'chocolate starfish.'"—Dr. Talley

"Trey was masturbating to *Juggs*. At least we know he's not gay."—Dr. Talley

Episode Sixteen: "Frenemies"

Q-tastic Trivia
Trey and Charlotte finally do it. Finally!

"Q"-uotes

"That girl needs the stick out of her ass and a dick in her coochie, pronto."—Samantha

"I mean don't you ever just want to be really pounded hard? You know, when the bed is moving all around and it's all sweaty and your head is knocking up against the headboard and you feel like it might just

The Men

Character	Actor	Slept with	Notes	You might know him from such gay-friendly films and shows as
Will			Miranda's date who stands her up because he dies	
Jim	Dominic Fumusa		Carrie's ex-, a friend of Will's, he dates Miranda despite Carrie's assertion that he's an asshole	
Sebastian		Samantha	They just fuck	

blow off? Dammit, I just really want to be fucked, you know? Just really fucked!"—Charlotte

---

Episode Seventeen: "What Goes Around Comes Around"

Q-tastic Trivia
Samantha and Carrie attend Sam Jones's party in Coulter Hall, and the episode is directed by Allen Coulter. It's kind of like what Hitchcock did, but more subtle.

Q-tastic Moment
Trey plays night tennis in his boxers. No direct connections to our community here, it's just nice to see.

The Men

Character	Actor	Slept with	Notes	You might know him from such gay-friendly films and shows as
Charles	Scott Geyer		Trey's brother	
Gardener	Steve Harris		The object of various fantasies, Charlotte is caught kissing him. By her sister-in-law	
Mugger	Brandon Fox		Steals Carrie's shoes	
Detective Stevens	Timothy Gibbs	Miranda	Gorgeous cop who thinks Miranda's an alcoholic	
Sam Jones	Jacob Pitts	Sam	College guy who shares Samantha's name, she decides to educate him	*Strangers with Candy*

"Q"-uotes

"What's the point of being in the suburbs if you're not going to fuck a gardener?"—Samantha

"Somebody stop him! He took my strappy sandals!" —Carrie

"I don't have any outfits that go with hunk."—Miranda

Episode Eighteen: "Cock A Doodle Do!"

Q-tastic Trivia

Carrie lives behind an animal hospital, where they keep
roosters on the roof. New Yorkers wonder if they've
claimed squatters' rights from the pigeons.

Flirtinis are made with vodka, pineapple, and champagne. We run to our liquor cabinets.

Miranda's address is 331 West 78th, apt 4F. Nice.

The Men

Character	Actor	Slept with	Notes	*You might know him from such gay-friendly films and shows as*
Guy	Jack Hartnett	Sam	Leaves in the middle of the night because of Samantha's tirade over the tranny hookers outside her window	
Destiny	Michael Jefferson		Tranny	Broadway: *Damage*
Chyna	T. Oliver Reid		Tranny	
Joe No E	Karen Covergirl		Tranny	

Aidan and Steve are friends. What?
First time the credits roll. Why?
End music: dancey "Flying Above the Clouds" Nice.

"Q"-uotes

- "Never say 'Cathy comic' to me again."—Carrie
- "Transexuals. Chicks with dicks. Boobs on top, balls down below?"—Samantha
- "I understand that pseudo-straight married men from New Jersey have to get laid, but do they have to do it on my block?"—Samantha

CHAPTER NINE

Profile: Cynthia Nixon

Q
QUOTE

We couldn't help but wonder . . .
what actress had enough S&M (sarcasm and Miranda) to make her B&D

CYNTHIA NIXON seems to have spent the better part of her professional life channeling the energy and attitude of her native New York into her acting roles. In true New Yorker type-A style, she played in two Broadway productions, David Rabe's *Hurlyburly* and Tom Stoppard's *The Real Thing* at the same time, necessitating her literally running from one theater to another. Nixon's Broadway-baby status and Q-appeal was boosted with her roles in Tony Kushner's *Angels in America* as well as Wendy Wasserstein's *The Heidi Chronicles*. One of the first actresses to owe her initial mass exposure to cable television, Nixon starred in *Tanner '88*, a mocku-mentary miniseries in which she played the daughter of a man running for president.

After years of television movies, television guest appearances, and films such as *The Pelican Brief* and *Marvin's Room*, her star rose to the stratosphere, again on cable, as our favorite sarcastic, pessimistic, yet undeniably hilarious and soft-on-the-inside lawyer, Miranda Hobbes. Though originally brought in to read for the role of Carrie, Nixon instinctively knew that she wasn't right for the part, but lobbied her manager to get her a role—any role—on the series, noting that the potential for the characters was both unprecedented and unlimited. Luckily for her, and us, she and her character seem to have been tailor-made for one another. Filled to the brim with sarcasm, humor, and an unerring sense of practical pessimism, Miranda's self-deprecation and practicality was continually undermined by her inherent sensitivity, fierce loyalty, and nurturing spirit.

Nixon's commitment to New York, is well known, and is matched by her commitment to the small independent plays and films that orginate in New York. A founding member (along with Sarah Jessica Parker and John Cameron Mitchell) of the off-Broadway theater troupe Drama Department, she starred, both during and after *Sex and the City*'s run, in a wonderful variety of small and independent films, such as *Little Manhattan* and *Igby Goes Down*. Once the show ended, Nixon went on to star in the Broadway revival of Claire Booth Luce's *The Women*, and in *Rabbit Hole*, for which she won a Tony Award. On television, she received numerous awards and widespread praise for

SEX AND THE SIDEBAR

Of all the scenes in *Sex and the City*, the one I remember the most took place in my beloved Brooklyn. Steve has just dragged Miranda to see a house, and she's thinking of every possible excuse not to buy it. Frustrated by her unwillingness to adapt to her changing family, he reminds her that the house, in fact every decision she makes from here on out, isn't just about her anymore. You can see the shift from Miranda the career-minded single woman to Miranda the wife and mother, as she watches Steve, Brady, and the dog playing in the backyard. I counted that as the moment when Miranda validated what a lot of us in the same situation were experiencing: confusion about the next step in our lives, and absolute terror about becoming someone we didn't know.

—LK, New Jersey, Publishing Executive
and Lost Tourist Guide

her portrayal of Eleanor Roosevelt in HBO's *Warm Springs*, and most recently, she gave a breathtaking and sure-to-be-Emmy-nominated performance on *Law & Order: SVU*.

Usually a private person, Nixon may have been surprised to find her personal life on the front pages when her relationship with her longtime partner and father of her children, ended. Her fans may have been even more surprised to hear that she replaced her partner with—a woman! In a 2006 interview with *New York* magazine, Nixon sums up her decision to admit her bisexuality and face the controversy surrounding it in the usual, no-nonsense, New Yorky way we've all come to admire from her. "There wasn't a struggle; there wasn't an attempt to suppress. I met this woman. I fell in love with her, and I'm a public figure." You go, girl!

In an ironic twist of art imitating life, or life imitating art, Nixon said that, like her character's friend, she was herself a breast cancer survivor, and proceeded to work to raise awareness of this devastating disease.

CHAPTER TEN

The Clothes

We couldn't help but wonder . . .
what's under the clothes?

THERE'S JUST something about absofuckinlutely fantastic about clothes. If you don't agree with this statement, then this chapter, if not this entire book, is not for you. For those of you left, I write again: There's just something absofuckinlutely fantastic about clothes. Clothes do, in fact, make the man. And the woman. And the man dressing like a woman. To paraphrase a certain mid-century matchmaker from Yonkers, put on your Sunday clothes when you feel down and out, and you'll feel as great as Carrie after a big, successful date.

New York native Patricia Field and her daughter, Rebecca Weinberg, were the geniuses who dressed our favorite New York quad each season. By mixing new and vintage pieces, they were able to define each of the character's personalities, allowing the actresses to fully flesh out their roles, and ushering in a whole new era in fashion. Would the world know the name Manolo Blahnik were it not for Carrie's obsession? Would gold name-plates, horseshoe necklaces, or short shorts have made their way into mainstream society? Probably not. In the show, you could tell, just by looking at them, that Charlotte, in her Shoshana and Moschino casual wear, is the more conservative and classic, that Samantha, in Emmanuel Ungaro pantsuits, Lulu Guiness hats, and Roberto Cavalli jeans is willing to put her strong personality out there, that Miranda has a need for a tailored life, with her preference for Bill Blass, Barneys, and Versus. And Carrie's willingness to wear mostly anything, ranging from a pinstriped Vivienne Westwood suit to an ensemble of cape, Prada skirt, Moschino shirt, and Chloe bustier, to her signature tutu, clearly indicates that this is a girl who's willing to try anything.

By choosing the best and most appropriate clothes with names like Chanel, Jacobs, and Dolce & Gabbana, Field and Weinberg created their own designs, scoured thrift shops, and selected pieces of couture that made grown men and women weep from their audaciousness, style, and fashion-forward sensibility.

Though each of the actresses now complain of foot and leg cramping as a result of the fabulous footwear they had to wear during filming, they all acknowledge that without Field's contributions, the show wouldn't have achieved the heights of critical and popular acclaim it did.

After *Sex and the City* ended, Field was nominated for five Emmy Awards, winning one, as well as six Costume Designer Awards, winning four, for her work on *Sex and the City*. Going on to design for the pilot of the next New

SEX AND THE SIDEBAR

When I was living in Manhattan, my friends and I would create *Sex and the City* "Wish Lists" in which we would write down and sketch what ever item(s) we saw on the most recent episode that were simply "must haves." Clothes, accessories, whatever. This was before the dawn of Tivo, mind you, so we had to write quickly. Every Monday, after we'd made sure we could read our notes, a gaggle of my gal pals and I would traipse from Barneys to Bendel's to Saks with sad little sketches in hand to see if we could locate and purchase what we saw. The funny thing was that we usually didn't even need the sketches; all we would have to do was mention *Sex and the City* and the salespeople would know exactly what we were looking for.

And yes, the first Cosmo I ever drank was because of Carrie. And yes, my friends and I would eat at a coffee shop every week because the girls did. I still miss that challah French toast.

—RK, Los Angeles, Entertainment Executive
and Persian Princess

York fashionista showcase, *Ugly Betty*, Field was nominated for an Academy Award for her costuming work on *The Devil Wears Prada*. A bone fide New York institution, her Q-icon status was guaranteed when she served as a guest judge, long before SJP, on perhaps the gayest show on television today, Bravo's *Project Runway*.

CHAPTER ELEVEN

Season Four

Episode 1: "The Agony and the Ex-tacy"

Q-tastic trivia

Big's phone number: 212-459-1905. I tried it. Someone yelled at me.

SJP becomes co-executive producer. If only Matthew Broderick starred in the *Co-Executive Producers*.

"Q"-uotes

"Trey, you have a boner. I can't discuss my notes if you have a boner."—Charlotte

"Soul mates only exist in the Hallmark aisle of Duane Reade Drugs."—Miranda

"Clooney's like a Chanel suit. He'll always be in style." —Carrie

"With no true soul mate, I spent the afternoon with shoe-sole mate: Manolo Blahnik."—Carrie

"Twenty-five? Fuck I'm old!"—Woman at restaurant

The Men

Character	Actor	Slept with	Notes	You might know him from such gay-friendly films and shows as
Danny	Jonathan Dokuchitz			*Anastasia, Pocahontas*
Phil	Yul Vazquez			*The F Word,* played gay guy on *Seinfeld*
Friar Fuck	Costas Mandylor			*Picket Fences*

Episode Two: "The Real Me"

Q-tastic Trivia

Charlotte was a teen model for Ralph Lauren in New Haven. We assume the Sears catalogue was already booked.

Q-tastic Moments

In what is perhaps the gayest episode ever, this one has more Q parts than a traveling Liberace exhibit. Real people being elevated to model-levels of beauty, fashion-as-drag, guest stars galore, a failed yet well-intentioned gay blind date, and underlying themes of self-love, friendship, survival, and the goddess-given right of everyone—*everyone*—to be fabulous.

Charlotte sets Stanford up with Anthony, because, well, they're both gay so why wouldn't they be perfect for each other, right? Unfortunately, Anthony quickly dismisses Stanford, rudely, because he's not up to his standards. A series-spanning catfight is born, and we're riveted to see how these two will carry on their animosity throughout the seasons.

Q-gasmic Guest Stars

Margaret Cho (*Notorious CHO, I'm the One That I Want*) as Lynne
Make-up artist Kevyn Aucoin as himself
Hairstylist Orlando Pita as himself
Heidi Klum (*Project Runway*) as herself
Mayor Ed Koch as himself

"Q"-uotes

"The only way I could get a guy like that interested in me is to pay him."—Stanford
"This is my 'boyfriend' Damian. I use the term 'boyfriend' loosely as Damian is clearly a homosexual."
—Lynne
"Sexy is the thing I try to get them to see me as after I win them over with my personality."—Miranda
"Ha, ha; it's so funny my vagina's depressed."
—Charlotte
"When I first moved to New York and I was totally broke, sometimes I would buy *Vogue* instead of dinner. I just felt it fed me more."—Carrie
"I've been rejected by someone I wasn't interested in. I hate when that happens."—Stanford
"She's fashion road-kill."—Stanford

The Men

Character	Actor	Slept with	Notes	You might know him from such gay-friendly films and shows as
O	Alan Cumming		Stylist we "likey"	Broadway: *Cabaret*, *The L Word*, *Spice World*, *Tin Man*, *Circle of Friends*, *Annie*, *X2*
Minion, O's assistant	Luca Calvani		O's assistant	
Damian	Jose Llana		Lynne's "boy-friend"	Broadway: *The King and I*, *Flower Drum Song*, *Spelling Bee*
Dave	Daniel Travis		Picks Miranda up at the gym, but is eventually turned off when she comes across as too full of herself	
Photographer	Jeff Forney		Photographs Samantha	
Tiger	Tony Hale		His assistant who can't keep his eyes off Samantha's body, and her comfort with it	*Arrested Development*
Paul	James McCaffrey		Photojournalist flirter who documents Carrie's rise and fall	
Delivery Guy	Adrian Martinez		Sees the photo hanging in her hallway and compliments Samantha's ass	

Episode Three: "Defining Moments"

Q-tastic Moment

Maria, yet another artist showing at Charlotte's gallery, played by Sonia Braga (*Kiss of the Spider Woman*, *Testosterone*). Samantha's open to it. So are we.

Q-gasmic Guest Star

Sonia Braga as Maria, a lesbian artist who shows at Charlotte's gallery and is immediately taken with Samantha

The Men

Character	Actor	Slept with	Notes	You might know him from such gay-friendly films and shows as
Big				
Ray	Craig Bierko	Carrie	ADD jazz guy	*Johns, Scary Movie 4*, Broadway: *The Music Man*
Trey				
Doug	Jim Gaffigan	Miranda	*New Yorker* cartoonist leaves door open during his bathroom activities	*The Ellen Show*

"Q"-uotes

"Who cares what you are? Just enjoy it."—Samantha
"An open-door dump was definitely worth dumping
   someone over."—Carrie

Episode Four: "What's Sex Got to Do with It?"

Q-tastic Moment

Proving that television can be educational as well as entertaining, Samantha discovers female ejaculation. Who knew? She didn't. Neither did many of us. The more you know . . .

"Q"-uotes

"Yes ladies, I'm a lesbian."—Samantha
"I don't think she's a lesbian. I think she just ran out of
   men."—Charlotte
"Vagina shmagina."—Samantha
"Trey, I'm on the mallard!"—Charlotte
"There are places a dick can't go."—Samantha
"I know you're probably having mind-blowing sex right
   now, but I feel that you need to know that your good
   friend Miranda Hobbes has just taken a piece of cake
   out of the garbage and eaten it. You'll probably need
   this information when you check me into the Betty
   Crocker clinic."—Miranda

Episode Five: "Ghost Town"

"Q"-uotes

"My dear child, you cannot not have a dust ruffle. It's
  unsightly."—Bunny
"It's like we live in the museum of natural ugliness."
  —Charlotte
"You bought me a strap-on?"—Samantha
"Would it be bad to have a martini with my muscle
  relaxant, or bad in a good way?"—Samantha

The Men

Character	Actor	Slept with	Notes	You might know him from such gay-friendly films and shows as
Brian	Chris Meyer		Some guy Samantha used to fuck	
Sean	Joe Petcka		Some guy Samantha used to fuck	

Episode Six: "Baby, Talk Is Cheap"

"Q"-uotes

"You gotta get online if only for the porn."—Samantha

"I finally had to sit on his face to shut him up."
    —Samantha

"There's something happening with men and the ass."
    —Samantha

The Men

Character	Actor	Slept with	Notes	You might know him from such gay-friendly films and shows as
Marathon Man	Michael Knowles	Miranda	Butt guy who wants Miranda to reciprocate	*Two Point Five*
Warren	John Bolger	Samantha	Baby talker who acts like a baby	*Black and White, Parting Glances*

Episode Seven: "Time and Punishment"

Q-tastic Trivia

Charlotte quits the gallery to devote her life to volunteerism, and to redecorating her apartment. She's quitting her job? But what about purpose? What about independence? What about the benefits? Oh, she's married to a rich, gorgeous man, and never has to lift a finger. Ok, we get it now.

"Q"-uotes

"We have to run to Helga the hot-waxer every other week, but them? How would they like it if we told them to shape their hedge, trim their trunk?"
—Samantha
"Every time I blow you I feel like I'm flossing."
—Samantha

The Men

Character	Actor	Slept with	Notes	You might know him from such gay-friendly films and shows as
Brad	Ted King	Samantha	Gets shaved by Samantha, realizes it makes him look bigger	

Episode Eight: "My Motherboard, My Self"

Q-tastic Trivia

Miranda's mother dies. I warned you.

Miranda's sister's name is Betsy. The other one doesn't count, which is just as well because this one sounds like a royal bitch.

"Q"-uotes

"When I RSVP to a party I make it my business to cum."—Samantha

"I didn't realize I needed a date for my mother's funeral."—Miranda

"The flowers were supposed to say 'We're so sorry, we love you,' not 'You're dead, let's disco.'"—Charlotte

The Men

Character	Actor	Slept with	Notes	*You might know him from such gay-friendly films and shows as*
Nick	Peter Onoratti	Samantha	Very flexible wrestling coach	Played gay on *American Dreams, ER, Ordinary Sinner*

Q-gasmic Guest Star:
Aasif Mandvi (*Oz*, Tanner on *Tanner* (with Cynthia Nixon!) Broadway: *Oklahoma!*)

Episode Nine: "Sex & the Country"

Q-tastic Trivia

Steve has testicular cancer. Lance Armstrong totally stole his thunder.

Steve's glasses disappear in the middle of his "thank you for being a bitch" speech. Hey, editors, it's called "continuity."

"Q"-uotes

"Darling, I'm juicy now."—Trey

"Everybody's getting it. It's the Tivo of cancers." —Miranda

"What is it about weekends now? I swear to God, every

The Men

Character	Actor	Slept with	Notes	*You might know him from such gay-friendly films and shows as*
Guy	Christian William	Samantha	Hot guy in her bed	
Young McDonald	Christopher Braden Jones	Samantha	Aidan's neighbor	

guy I fuck since Memorial Day wants to know what I'm doing this weekend. They just don't get it. My weekends are for meeting new guys, so I don't have to keep fucking the old ones."—Samantha

"A squirrel is just a rat with a cuter outfit."—Carrie

"City girls are just country girls with better outfits." —Carrie

"I'd like a cheeseburger, a large fries, and a Cosmopolitan."—Carrie

"Nature and me? It's unnatural."—Carrie

Episode Ten: "Belles of the Balls"

"Q"-uotes

"Balls are to men what purses are to women. It's just a little bag, but we'd feel naked in public without it." —Carrie

The Men

Character	Actor	Slept with	Notes	You might know him from such gay-friendly films and shows as
Allan	Jack Gwaltney		Used to fuck Samantha, designed a hotel for Richard	
Richard	James Remar		Hotelier who won't hire Samantha because she's a woman	*Cruising*

"Charlotte, I'm eating. Is it too much to ask to have my moo shoo without a side of sperm?"—Trey

Episode Eleven: "Coulda, Woulda, Shoulda"

Q-tastic Moment

Samantha is so desperate to get a Birkin that she's willing to use a client's name, thereby harming her career, to get it. Though this is a little extreme, we've all been willing to risk something important for something frivolous (not that a Birkin is frivolous). We've all taken an

The Men

Character	Actor	Slept with	Notes	You might know him from such gay-friendly films and shows as
Hermes clerk	Craig Chester		Puts Samantha on the list for a Birkin once she uses Lucy Liu's name	*Adam & Steve*, *Boys Life 4*, *Kiss Me, Guido*, *Anonymous*, *Out on the Edge*, *Quintessence*, *The Look*, *Bumping Heads*, *Circuit*, *Charlie!*, *David Searching*, *Frisk*, *Grief*, author of *Why the Long Face*

extra long lunch because of a sample sale, or over-tipped the incompetent but sweet waiter. We've all lingered a little too long at the copier because of the cute technician fixing the jam, and we've all come "this close" to hiring, or firing, the underling who's just too damn cute.

Q-gasmic Guest Star

Lucy Liu (Charlie's Angels, Ally McBeal) as herself, hires Samantha to handle her public relations and styling.

"Q"-uotes

"He only has one ball and I have a lazy ovary. It's like the Special Olympics of conception."—Miranda

"It's not a bag. It's a Birkin."—Clerk

Episode Twelve: "Just Say Yes"

"Q"-uotes

"If you're going to ruin our lives, I'd at least like to look at a nice piece of jewelry."—Samantha

"If there were unlimited apartments in Manhattan we'd all be single forever."—Miranda

"Apparently we've reached the stage when our lives are making us sick."—Carrie

The Men

Character	Actor	Slept with	Notes	*You might know him from such gay-friendly films and shows as*
Richard		Samantha		

Episode Thirteen: "The Good Fight"

Q-tastic Trivia

No more World Trade Center in the opening credits.
If you slow down your DVD, you can see Richard's
   privates—three times—during the rooftop scene. It's
   the first male full-frontal of the series. I made sure to
   watch this over and over again for you, dear reader,
   just to make sure you have all the necessary information. You're welcome. And thank you.

"Q"-uotes

"This is why I've never lived with a man. This, and the
   fact that I want them out an hour after climax."
   —Samantha
"He's got the most perfect dick I've ever seen. Long.
   Pink. Amazing. It's dickalicious."—Samantha
"Don't do that. Don't mock the clothes."—Carrie
"I used to think those people who sat alone at Starbucks
   writing on their laptops were pretentious poseurs.

The Men

Character	Actor	Slept with	Notes	You might know him from such gay-friendly films and shows as
Walker	Robert John Burke	Miranda	Miranda uses him as her "last meal" before she becomes too obviously pregnant to have sex with anyone	*Connie and Carla, Oz*

Now I know they're people who recently moved in with someone."—Carrie

Episode Fourteen: "All that Glitters"

Q-tastic Moments

For a night on the town, the ladies go to a place where they know they'll have a great time: a gay bar. Let's face it, we throw the best parties, concoct the best cocktails, and have the best dance music. Some stereotypes are true. Let's enjoy this one!

It's a great moment when Miranda, who has a secret, runs into a colleague at the gay bar during the girls' night out. The colleague obviously isn't out at work. They bond over their shared secrets, but when he later outs her to the office gossip, she has no choice but to out him as well. Of course, he's the guy who ruins casual Fridays for everyone. He finds it perfectly acceptable to come to work in club wear. We all know at least one guy like that, don't we? If you don't, then you're that guy.

Every gay man has at least one straight, single, female friend. She's there to listen to our tales of woe, to accompany us to parties, and to go shopping with us when our gay friends just become too much. So when Stanford gets jealous of the time Carrie is spending with her new gay friend, we completely understand where he's coming from, including all the confusion. Is he jealous of her? Of *him*? Of their relationship? Does it matter? No! The fact of the matter is that our girl friends are ours and ours alone. It's not a traditional or logical relationship, but it's what we have. We like it. They like it. Do not get in our way.

"Q"-uotes

"Gay men have the possibility of sex at the gym. If straight men had that, they'd be working out all the time."—Carrie

"That afternoon I was high on another feel-good drug: the New Gay Friend."—Carrie

"I am not in the mood for gay porn."—Charlotte

"Gay men understand what's important. Clothes, compliments, and cocks."—Samantha

"Gay boyfriends are the loophole of monogamy."
   —Carrie

The Men

Character	Actor	Slept with	Notes	You might know him from such gay-friendly films and shows as
Gordon	Chris Payne Gilbert	Anthony's friend who works for *House & Garden*	again!	
Oliver	Murray Bartlett		Shoe importer, amd new gay friend of Carrie's	*Postmortem*
Max	Daniel Serafini Sauli	Miranda's coworker who she outs		

"I've been so preoccupied with my gay boyfriend, I kept forgetting about my gay husband."—Carrie

"You wore pink Candies and I adored you anyway."
    —Stanford

Episode Fifteen: "Change of a Dress"

Q-tastic Trivia

Susan Sharon returns. As annoying as her character is, the actress is so much better on *Bionic Woman*. Seriously, she is.

The Men

Character	Actor	Slept with	Notes	You might know him from such gay-friendly films and shows as
JJ	Marc Grapey	Samantha	Gossip columnist who can't get it up in the bathroom of a party	*Veronica's Closet*
Pat	Andre de Shields		Charlotte's dance instructor	Broadway: *The Wiz* ('74 and '93), *Ain't Misbehavin, The Full Monty, Play On!*

"Q"-uote

"I think I have monogamy. I must have caught it from you people."—Samantha

Episode Sixteen: "Ring a Ding Ding"

"Q"-uotes

"I'll be a bag lady. A Fendi bag lady, but a bag lady."
    —Carrie

Roger, honey, you've seen my bush. We're a little past acting coy."—Samantha

The Men

Character	Actor	Slept with	Notes	You might know him from such gay-friendly films and shows as
Roger	Robert Gomes		Richard's personal shopper	

Episode Seventeen: "A 'Vogue' Idea"

Q-tastic Trivia

Carrie's father left her family when she was little. That bastard.

The Men

Character	Actor	Slept with	Notes	You might know him from such gay-friendly films and shows as
Julian	Ron Rifkin		Father figure editor at Vogue	Brothers and Sisters, The Substance of Fire, Dress Gray

Q-gasmic Guest Stars

Ron Rifkin (*Soap, Alias, Brothers & Sisters,* Broadway:
  Cabaret)
Candace Bergen (*Murphy Brown, Boston Legal*)

"Q"-uotes

"Ladies, can we cut the cake and get out of here? I have
  a three-way to get to."—Samantha
"I thought these were an urban shoe myth."—Carrie

Episode 18: "I Heart NY"

Q-tastic Trivia
The first episode to be produced after September 11, this
show bears a heart-wrenching, and heartwarming ded-

The Men

Character	Actor	Slept with	Notes	You might know him from such gay-friendly films and shows as
Eric	Terry Maratos		Freaks out at the size of Charlotte's apartment	

ication: "Dedicated to our City of New York. Then, Now, and Forever."

"Q"-uote

"I'm always surprised when people leave New York. I mean, where do they go?"—Samantha

CHAPTER TWELVE

Profile: Kristin Davis

> We couldn't help but wonder . . .
> What woman had the right balance of sugar, spice, and everything naughty?

WE ALL know that the only way we'd believe someone could be as optimistic and hopeful as Charlotte York MacDougal Goldenblatt was if the part was played by an actress who first gained attention as a psychotic.

As *Melrose Place*'s over-the-top, manipulative, and Andrew Sue–obsessed Brooke, Kristin Davis's Q-appeal was guaranteed.

The Colorado native moved to New York in 1987, but appears to have never lost her Midwestern pluck. Davis's role could easily have degenerated into a sickeningly sweet caricature, but with a wide-eyed and seemingly true-to-life belief in romance and happiness, Davis was able to imbue the part with genuine depth and emotion. Often disappointed, but rarely deterred, Charlotte was our one ray of hope throughout the series' six seasons. She believed, so we believed. In fact, it was her optimism that prompted Carrie to dedicate her book to her, and us to keep rooting for her.

We were devastated when her marriage failed, but rallied around her when she summoned enough strength to challenge her prenuptial agreement. We suffered along with her as she struggled to have a baby, but melted as she shared her love with not only her husband, but also with her adopted religion and, always, with her dear friends. Charlotte is the friend we want around when we're having a bad day, the one who will let us grouse, and who will always be there to pick up our mail and rally our ex-boyfriends to rescue us from a doomed relationship.

After *Sex and the City*'s end, Davis went on to star as the voice of an animated spider in *Miss Spider's Sunny Patch Friends*, and in family-friendly films like *The Adventures of Shark Boy and Lava Girl in 3D*. She worked with Indie auteur Robert Rodriguez on *The Shaggy Dog*, and to keep it in the family, starred as Matthew Broderick's wife in *Deck the Halls*.

Usually private, her Charlotte-like sensibility came to the forefront when she revealed that she was, at the beginning of the series, uncomfortable with some of the language. And, like Charlotte, she's optimistic about the future. "If I had one wish for myself," she said, "it would be to fall in love. That's asking for trouble, but that's the truth."

CHAPTER THIRTEEN

He's Just Not That Into You

QUOTE

We couldn't help but
wonder . . .
Is a catch phrase just another name for a pickup
line?

LOTS OF catchphrases enter the vernacular of popular culture. "Shwing," "Don't have a cow, man," "Duh," "Where's the beef?" . . . the list is almost endless. But few catchphrases start a movement.

"He's just not that into you" did just that. Featured in Season Six's fourth episode, it's Berger's way of providing a male perspective on Miranda's dating confusion, and it served as a wakeup call for America.

The line, attributed to Greg Behrendt and Liz Tuccillo, a consultant to and writer for the show, the phrase cut through all the bull that women tell themselves, and

SEX AND THE SIDEBAR

After a few seasons of religiously watching *Sex and the City*, I resolved to stop worrying about whether or not shoes were comfortable. The ladies all looked so great in their stylish, spiky heels. I mean if they could do it, why couldn't I? When the show went off the air I was somewhat relieved. It gave me the chance to regroup, and remind myself that the show was a comedy, not a documentary. With the psychological pressure off, I decided to do something about the physical pressure, and went back to practical footwear, like clogs. I may not be dating as much, but I've never been happier.

—NK, New York, Marketing Director
and Well-heeled New Yorker

called men's actions to task. Basically, the phrase says that no man is too busy to call you back. No man is too wrapped up in personal drama to not treat you well. No man would treat someone he cares about poorly. And if he does? Well, then he's just not that into you. If he's into you, he'll call you back. If he's into you, he won't forget your birthday. If he's into you, he'll treat you like the goddess (or god) that you are.

Simple, clear, and entirely unexpected, the phrase, and the book it spawned, enlightened a generation of women about the true meaning of men's behavior, and put men on notice. The book's full title is *He's Just Not That Into You: The No-Excuses Truth to Understanding Guys*, and it shines a harsh light indeed on the psychology of the male of the species. Written by Behrendt and Tuccillo, it was published in 2004 to great acclaim, and quickly became a *New York Times* bestseller. Oprah featured the book and its authors twice, blasting sales into the stratosphere, and giving Behrendt and Tuccillo national exposure, which is something not every writer gets.

Behrendt went on to write another book, this time with his wife, and to host his own talk show, while Tuccillo went on to create the series *Related*.

CHAPTER FOURTEEN

Season Five

Episode One: "Anchors Away"

Q-tastic Trivia

Sjp becomes Executive Producer. If only Matthew . . . but you're getting tired of that, aren't you?

Q-tastic Moment

Fleet Week. Two words that make every straight woman and gay man in New York stand up and salute. There's nothing quite like seeing the streets of Manhattan teeming with men in their dress whites. They hold doors open for you. The look around The City in farm-boy wonder. They politely ask for directions and then appreciatively thank you for your help. They travel in groups of three or more, allowing you to fantasize that you've been dropped into a real-life version of *On the Town*. They wear those cute white pants that hug the right parts, and will sometimes allow you to hug the right parts as long as you "don't ask, don't tell."

Q-gasmic Guest Stars

Chandra Wilson (*Grey's Anatomy*) as a police officer
  who lets Samantha paper the neighborhood with
  anti-Richard signs
Sylvia Miles (*Urban Cowboy*) as a woman Carrie meets
  at a deli who likes to flavor her ice cream with anti-
  depressants

The Men

Character	Actor	Slept with	Notes	You might know him from such gay-friendly films and shows as
Louis	Daniel Sunjata		Sailor who invites Carrie to a party	*The Devil Wears Prada, Brother to Brother*, Broadway: *Take Me Out*
Sailors	Jamie Gustis			*Trick*
	Diego Lopez			*The Absolution of Anthony*
	Seth Cosentino		Now known as Seth Gabel.	*Dirty Sexy Money, Nip/Tuck*
	Mark Deklin			*Desperate Housewives*

"Q"-uotes

"You're never alone in New York. It's the perfect place to be single. The City is your date."—Carrie

"Breakups—bad for the heart, good for the economy." —Carrie

"You are so not gay."—Anthony

Episode Two: "Unoriginal Sin"

Q-tastic Trivia

Miranda says it's the first time she's heard of Steve's mother, but it isn't. Don't you feel superior now? Didn't this book just pay for itself?

Q-gasmic Guest Stars

Molly Shannon (*Saturday Night Live, Superstar, Year of the Dog*) as Lily, Carrie's publisher

Amy Sedaris (*Strangers with Candy, Shrek 3,* author of *I Like You*) as Courtney, Carrie's editor

Anne Meara (Ben Stiller's mother, *Archie Bunker's Place, Oz*) as Steve's mother, Mary

Episode Three: "Luck Be an Old Lady"

"Q"-uotes

"Most dates are like job interviews with cocktails."
   —Carrie
"Cleavage is big here. It's part of the regional charm."
   —Carrie

Episode Four: "Cover Girl"

Q-gasmic Guest Star
Judy Gold (out comedienne) as B&N clerk

"Q"-uotes

"We all judge. That's our hobby. Some people do arts
   and crafts. We judge."—Stanford
"I will not be judged by you or society. I will wear
   whatever I want and blow whomever I want as long as
   I can breathe and kneel."—Samantha

The Men

Character	Actor	Slept with	Notes	*You might know him from such gay-friendly films and shows as*
Worldwide Express Guy	Nick Scotti	Samantha	blows him in her office	*Kiss Me, Guido*
Tom	Craig Gass	Miranda	Weight Watchers stress eater, he's a bit sloppy in bed	
Marcus	Sean Palmer	Stanford	Broadway-caliber dancer, new boyfriend	*Grey's Anatomy, Chicago*
Photographer	Michael Zeppetello			

Episode Five: "Plus One is the Loneliest Number"

"Q"-uotes

"In New York, they say you're always looking for a job, a boyfriend, or an apartment."—Carrie

"That's the key to having it all. Stop expecting it to look like what you thought it would look like. That's true of the new fall lines, and it's true of relationships." —Enid

"The gay guy is the single gal's safety net."—Carrie

Q-gasmic Guest Stars

Patricia Field (*Sex and the City*'s costume designer) at
    book party
Isaac Mizrahi (designer, television host) attends Carrie's
    book party
HBO crossover: Dominic Chianese, Jr., is Gray's Papaya
    guy; his father plays Uncle Junior on *The Sopranos*

The Men

Character	Actor	Slept with	Notes	You might know him from such gay-friendly films and shows as
Berger	Ron Livingston			*Beat*
Walker		Miranda	Miranda's last meal comes back, this time overshadowed by Brady	
Justin	Peter Giles	Charlotte	Bunny scares him away	*Queer Eye for the Homeless Guy*
Gray's Papaya Guy	Dominic Chianese, Jr.	Gives Carrie and the limo driver free food to congratulate her for her book deal		

Episode Six: "Critical Condition"

Q-gasmic Guest Stars

Mary Testa (Broadway's *Xanadu, On the Town, A Funny Thing Happened on the Way to the Forum*) as cabaret singer

Heather Graham (*Boogie Nights, Scrubs*) as herself

Nadia Dajani (*Flirting with Disaster*) as Nina Katz, who dated Aidan after Carrie

Lisa Gay Hamilton (*The Practice*) as Kendall, Miranda's neighbor

The Men

Character	Actor	Slept with	Notes	You might know him from such gay-friendly films and shows as
Harry	Evan Handler		Charlotte's divorce lawyer's partner. She switches to him once she realizes that she can't be aggressive in front of the one she finds attractive	*Six Feet Under, CBS Afterschool Special: What if I'm Gay?*

"Q"-uotes

"I hadn't been up this early since Princess Diana's wedding."—Carrie

"You can't call a baby an asshole."—Carrie

"Sharper Image doesn't sell vibrators. It's a neck massager."—Clerk

Episode Seven

"The Big Journey"

"Q"-uotes

- "I've always wanted to take a train. It's so sexy. You never know who's going to be getting on, or getting me off."—Samantha
- "You're spelling 'sex' in a place with go-go boys on the bar?"—Anthony
- "Ugly sex is hot."—Anthony

The Men

Character	Actor	Slept with	Notes	You might know him from such gay-friendly films and shows as
Harry	Evan Handler	Charlotte		

Episode Eight: "I Love a Charade"

Q-tastic Moment

Gayer-than-gay Bobby Fine gets married. To a woman. Is lack of sexual attraction necessarily a relationship-killer, or when you fall in love with a person, do you just fall in love with a person? Is it as possible for a gay man to genuinely fall in love with a woman as it is for a "straight" man to "turn" gay? Why not? Who are we to judge?

Q-gasmic Guest Stars

Nathan Lane (Broadway: *The Producers, Guys and Dolls, Love! Valour! Compassion!,* Film: *The Producers, The Birdcage*) as Bobby Fine

Julie Halston (Broadway: *Gypsy, The Women,* with Cynthia Nixon) as Bitsy

"Q"-uotes

"Just when you thought you'd never hear a phrase gayer than 'Mr. Broadway has to tinkle.'"—Miranda

"Not having sex was the only thing holding our relationship together."—Miranda

"I revealed too much to soon. I was emotionally slutty."—Carrie

"She can marry a gay guy, but you can't marry an Episcopalian?"—Charlotte

CHAPTER FIFTEEN

The Syndicated Series

We couldn't help but wonder . . .
what the F**k is with the censors?

ONE OF the ways television shows, meaning the producers of television shows, make money is through the magic of syndication. And though most series that appear on commercial or network television require little to no editing (other than for time to allow for additional commercial breaks), series that appear in other countries or on cable or pay television, meaning those shows that don't adhere to the normal Federal Communications Commission (FCC) standards and practices of network programming, need significant cuts for content. Now pretty much anything goes on cable, and the reins of what can and can't be said or shown on broadcast television have been loosened over the past few years. The older generations can remember when you couldn't show a married couple in a bed together, or say the word "pregnant," but today we can all hear an unprecedented number of once-naughty words, and we can see extreme acts of violence and sex during countless pre- and prime-time hours. How on earth could *Sex and the City*, with language bawdy enough to make one of those sailors blush (see "Anchors Away," Season Five, Episode One) and with its breast-baring, cunnilingis-simulating, orgasm-celebrating sexual content ever be shown on commercial television or basic cable? As it turns out, surprisingly easily.

Perhaps it is because of the quickly-changing standards of society, or that it is just impossible to suck the life out of something so incredibly rich, but the necessarily toned-down, broadcast-appropriate *Sex and the City* has been able to retain the majority of its charm and content. Like Times Square after the "Disneyfica-tion" clean-up, you can water down the series, but you can't dampen its underlying spirit. Viewers used to watching the show on HBO or on DVDs will undoubt-edly notice that when the show is re-broadcast on local stations that some lines of dialogue are dubbed over to remove any offensive language. Exposed body parts, usu-ally Samantha's breasts, or overtly sexual situations, usually Samantha's going down on someone, are trimmed (like Samantha's lady parts) with the use of quick-cuts to other scenes, or commercial breaks (usu-ally for lady products). These edits do tend to be a little jarring, especially when you know what's coming (or in the case of Vaughn, coming too soon). Though you can sort of "get" what happened between the time Vaughn and Carrie are making out and the time Carrie's telling the girls about it, the fact that you can't see Vaughn nor Carrie's reaction to him robs the scene of some emotional depth.

When watching a re-broadcast, don't count on seeing any of the girls having sex as graphic as you're used to. Though you'll still enjoy Charlotte's gardener's body in as much detail as you want, you'll miss seeing Richard's package during his rooftop skinny-dip with Samantha. And though the girls' Tantric sex workshop retains the majority of its educational content, it, and we, suffer from the loss of its money shot (though I'm sure Miranda is fine with not being splashed in the face with semen). Some of the cuts really do reduce the impact of the show, especially those of particularly dramatic moments, like Charlotte's struggling to literally get back on a horse, and the touching, series-finale moment between Magda and Miranda.

If you look and listen closely, episodes can actually be time compressed, too, so the perfect timing that worked so well on cable is now just a little . . . off. Coffee shop banter on re-broadcast often comes at a *West Wing*-like pace, but the biggest tragedy is that the awkward, painful silences are just a hairsbreadth shorter. It is a testament to the skills of the writers, actors, and original editors that you can actually feel a change from just a few fleeting, shaved-off moments. I guarantee that you will have a consciously different emotional and intellectual reaction to the show depending on whether you see the original or a re-broadcast.

Sex and the City can now be seen, in addition to the re-broadcast, on demand, and on DVD sets here in

SEX AND THE SIDEBAR

My favorite *Sex and the City* character is Marcus, Stanford's handsome boyfriend. Though he was never given many lines, his impossibly beautiful face and perfect body draw your attention. To me, he is the main character of every scene he is in. I couldn't wait to see how Marcus would react to each of the other characters' antics, but more importantly, how would they react to *him*?

Romantic fantasy, of course, is the animating force of this TV series. So, why shouldn't the gay love interest be a dreamy confection named Marcus?

Interestingly, right after the *Sex and the City* finale, I saw Sean Palmer, the actor who played Marcus, in a Hamptons stage production of *The Boyfriend*, directed by beloved Broadway icon Julie Andrews. Mr. Palmer proved himself a delightful and accomplished singer, dancer, and actor. It was pretty obvious that every eye in the theater was focused only on this talented young actor, who was perfection as the love interest of central character Miss Polly Browne. I have to admit that I wrote Sean Palmer a fan letter afterwards.

Will Marcus be in the movie? Or, more importantly, will he have his own feature film?

—SF, New York, Literary Agent and Gadabout

the United States and in over fifty countries around the world. Now people in such diverse countries as Latvia, Denmark, Macedonia, Finland, and Croatia can take advantage of the weak American dollar and visit New

York searching for their own pair of Manolos. Or their own Big!

Yet despite these changes, thanks to syndication, the series is now as ubiquitous on television and in the greater American consciousness as *The Golden Girls* and *Everybody Loves Raymond*. Sure, the language is cleaned up and the scenes aren't as graphic, but you still can't help but fall in love with these women, and their New York, over and over again. No FCC rules and regulations can compromise the integrity of the characters, or change their world enough to really matter. It is the essence of the show, not to mention the fabulous shoes, which will keep us sitting through the commercials.

CHAPTER SIXTEEN

Season Six, Part One

Episode One: "To Market, To Market"

Q-tastic Trivia

Carrie takes the subway! We knew she knew about it, but the closest she ever came was the bus. And the bus is, like, above ground. Wow.

Harry tells Charlotte he loves her. Single Jewish women around New York gasp as yet another shiksa goddess steals a nice Jewish boy from them.

Q-tastic Moments

Aidan has a baby (who is played by SJP's real-life baby), proving that any man, even already hot men, look even hotter with a baby.

Samantha walks home, past her neighborhood sex club, the RamHole, and though she doesn't pay attention to the guys in assless chaps, or the leather-hooded, leashed man kneeling by his master, she's taken aback by the sign touting the arrival of a Pottery Barn.

Q-gasmic Guest Star
Wallace Langham (*Veronica's Closet*) as Willy

"Q"-uotes

"There's more to being a Jew than jewelry."—Charlotte
"I love the stock market. A room of screaming, sweaty men trying to get it up."—Samantha

The Men

Character	Actor	Slept with	Notes	You might know him from such gay-friendly films and shows as
Berger	Ron Livingston		Writer of a not very successful book who Carrie meets in her publisher's office	
Chip	Victor Webster	Samantha	Stockbroker neighbor who gets arrested for insider trading while they're having sex	*Noah's Arc, Emily's Reasons Why Not*

"If you think I'm overreacting here, you should be
    inside my head."—Miranda
"What kind of man passes pussy for Purim?"
    —Samantha

Episode Two: "Great Sexpectations"

"Q"-uotes

"I'd like him to amuse my bouche."—Samantha
"Fuck me badly once, shame on you. Fuck me badly
    twice, shame on me."—Samantha
"When it comes to sex, spray it, don't say it."
    —Samantha

The Men

Character	Actor	Slept with	Notes	You might know him from such gay-friendly films and shows as
Jerry	Jason Lewis	Samantha	Waiter at a raw food restaurant	Played gay on *Brothers & Sisters*

Episode Three: "The Perfect Present"

Q-gasmic guest star

Jennifer Coolidge (Broadway: *The Women*, Film: *Best in Show*, *Legally Blonde*, *For Your Consideration*) as Victoria

"Q"-uotes

"Who needs a balding 38-year-old boyfriend with erectile dysfunction when you can an have a new career and cute cater waiters?"—Victoria
"There's no polite way to get out of phone sex."—Carrie
"Oh God. There goes my hard-on."—Samantha

Episode Four: "Pick-a-little, Talk-a-Little"

Q-tastic Trivia

"He's Just Not That into You" becomes a rallying cry across America. Oprah listens.
Carrie and Berger say they love each other. Berger, in turn, like most men, will prove unworthy of her love. Men suck.

The Men

Character	Actor	Slept with	Notes	You might know him from such gay-friendly films and shows as
Paul	Nick Gregory		Has to admit to Miranda that he can't continue the date because he has diarrhea	*The Night Listener*

"Q"-uotes

"It's so refreshing to be with someone who likes to fuck outside the box." —Samantha

"The best part of a night out with your friends is talking about them on the way home."—Carrie

"Sass'll bite you in the ass."—Miranda

Episode Five: "Lights, Camera, Relationship"

"Q"-uotes

"Nice day to get laid."—Anthony

"I'm not usually a fan of the theater, but get your cock out."—Samantha

The Men

Character	Actor	Slept with	Notes	*You might know him from such gay-friendly films and shows as*
Tony from Prada	William Abadie		Tries to get Berger to buy a shirt	*Ugly Betty*

Episode Six: "Hop, Skip, and a Week"

Q-gasmic Guest Star
Doris Belack (*The Golden Girls*, *Tootsie*) as Lenore

"Q"-uotes

"Macaroons on the outside, dear."—Lenore

The Men

Character	Actor	Slept with	Notes	*You might know him from such gay-friendly films and shows as*
David	Peter Hermann		Charlotte's boring set-up date	Married to TV's Mariska Hargitay
Jonathan	David Pittu		Charlotte's gay set-up date	"Harry" in *Company* on Broadway

"I knew it was going to be terrible. The man brought me
carnations."—Charlotte

"First come the gays, then the girls, then the industry."—Samantha

---

Episode Seven: "The Post-It Always Sticks Twice"

"Q"-uotes

"If you're never someone's girlfriend, you're never
someone's ex-girlfriend."—Samantha

"You are going to be the fantasy of every adolescent girl
and sexually confused boy in America."—Samantha

The Men

Character	Actor	Slept with	Notes	You might know him from such gay-friendly films and shows as
Peter	Brent Crawford		Guy at Bed who flirts with Miranda, restoring her confidence	
Billy	Michael Showalter		Berger's friend who gets the brunt of Carrie's rage at the way Berger broke up with her	*Kissing Jessica Stein*, *Wet Hot American Summer*

"That's exactly what my mind needs: cloudiness."
   —Carrie
"Very few women can pull off anger in a tube-top."
   —Samantha

Episode Eight: "The Catch"

"Q"-uotes

"Wouldn't you rather be at Jeffrey? They're having a sale on stripes."—Stanford

"Women and candles have replaced women and cats as the new, sad thing."—Samantha

"You are insane for getting into a harness without even the hope of an orgasm."—Samantha

The Men

Character	Actor	Slept with	Notes	You might know him from such gay-friendly films and shows as
Howie	Bryan Callen	Carrie	Harry's best man whose jackhammer style throws Carrie's back out	*Fat Actress, Oz*

"I'm having a Jewish wedding and I look like Hitler."
   —Charlotte
"He's a regular jerk-du-soleil."—Carrie

Episode Nine: "A Woman's Right to Shoes"

Q-gasmic Guest Star

Tatum O'Neal (*Paper Moon*, *Little Darlings*, *Wicked Wicked Games*) as Kyra, who throws a party where Carrie's shoes are stolen

"Q"-uotes

"I played "William Wants a Doll" so many times I almost turned my little sister into a gay man."
   —Stanford
"Oh, I thought you meant tea bagging—when you hold a guy's ball in your mouth."—Samantha

The Men

Character	Actor	Slept with	Notes	You might know him from such gay-friendly films and shows as
Robert	Blair Underwood		Miranda's new neighbor	

Episode Ten: "Boy, Interrupted"

Q-tastic Trivia

Charlotte was prom queen and a cheerleader. Isn't that nice?

Marcus was an escort. You thought he looked familiar, didn't you?

Q-tastic Moment

Stanford is involved in the planning of the Gay Prom at the LGBT Center. Many of us never had the prom experience our straight friends enjoyed—or suffered through. While their expectations of romance and magic were either met or comically deferred, we spent our evenings trying to pretend to be something we weren't, making the best of an awkward situation, or just staying home watching television with our parents. Gay proms have popped up all over the country, finally giving us the nights we've been waiting for.

Q-gasmic Guest Stars

David Duchovny (*X-Files*, *Californication*) as Jeremy, Carrie's high school sweetheart

Writer and director Michael Patrick King as an un-credited "Feces!"-screaming mental patient

Drag queen and New York nightlife fixture, The Lady
   Bunny, serves as MC of the gay prom.

"Q"-uotes

"My fictional plans fell through, so I'm available."
   —Carrie
"That's Chelsea for you. Can't swing a dick without
   running into someone you know."—Anthony
"Wake up and smell the KY."—Anthony
"I don't want to hear the truth from some bitchy queen
   with back issues of *Honcho*."—Stanford
"Anything is possible. This is New York."—Carrie

The Men

Character	Actor	Slept with	Notes	You might know him from such gay-friendly films and shows as
Robert		Miranda		
Jeremy	David Duchovny	Carrie	Carrie's high school sweetheart, now a patient at a local mental hospital	*Queer Duck: The Movie, Trust the Man, Connie and Carla,* played sort of gay on *The Larry Sanders Show*

Episode Eleven: "The Domino Effect"

Q-tastic trivia

Bitsy's pregnant, and Bobby's the father! And they say the age of miracles has passed.

Episode Twelve: "One"

"Q"-uotes

"Nothing's scarier than a clown."—Carrie

"I have a sexy young man who loves to fuck me, and I'm fabulous."—Samantha

"My nipples are hard just thinking about him." —Samantha

"Smith enjoys a full bush."—Samantha

"I am so fucked up. I am so fucked up."—Miranda

"No man wants to fuck Grandma's pussy."—Samantha

Q-tastic Trivia

Samantha is 45. We never would have guessed.

When you're feeling down and out, nothing brings you out of your funk like *Elizabeth Taylor: The E! True Hollywood Story*. And isn't that the truth? I mean if Elizabeth Taylor can survive Hollywood, a crush on a crashed gay guy, a billion medical issues, weight

The Men

Character	Actor	Slept with	Notes	*You might know him from such gay-friendly films and shows as*
Aleksandr	Mikhail Baryshnikov	Russian artist		

issues, and a marriage to something named Larry Fortensky, while still managing to raise millions of dollars for AIDS and look fabulous all the while, who the heck are we to complain about having a bad day? Look to La Liz, people. For she will show us the way.

Nice and Easy hair coloring, when left on too long, turns pubic hair orange. You may not want to try that at home.

CHAPTER SEVENTEEN

Season Six, Part Two

Episode One: "Let There Be Light"

"Q"-uotes

"I'll give you a hundred dollars if you say something bitchy about someone we know."—Anthony

"Why, why, why did I have to shit where I eat?" —Miranda

"Making pancakes for pussy? That's a classy touch." —Samantha

"Sometimes I don't know whether to blow him or burp him."—Samantha

Episode Two: "The Ick Factor"

Q-tastic Trivia

Miranda proposes to Steve. Brady is finally legit. Samantha has cancer. Oh crap.

Q-gasmic Guest Star

Heather MacRae (Film: *Everything You Always Wanted to Know About Sex but Were Afraid to Ask, Clarissa Explains It All,* Broadway: *Falsettos, Hair*) as the judge presiding over Miranda and Steve's marriage

"Q"-uotes

"I think it's romantic if someone offers me a seat on the subway."—Carrie

"One of the great things about living in New York City is that you don't have to sugar-coat your feelings." —Carrie

"I'm an American. You gotta take it down a notch." —Carrie

Episode Three: "Catch-38"

Q-tastic Moment

One of the central themes of this episode concerns the issue of whether what we want matches up to what we, or other people, think we should want. In this case, Steve wants a quiet, romantic honeymoon, and the girls think Miranda should want it, but Miranda doesn't. Isolated and forced into a weekend without television, limited cell phone reception, and constant relaxation, she's forced to confront the fact that what she wants doesn't necessarily match with what she, her husband, and friends expect from her. Isn't this what the gay community goes through? Many of us are told, from a very early age, that we should want to get married to a member of the opposite sex and have children and a dog. But part of accepting yourself, and others, is recognizing that by forcing yourself to do what others want and expect will only lead into an unfulfilled life, filled with compromise, and lacking in any true satisfaction or happiness.

Q-gasmic Guest Star

Julia Sweeney (*Saturday Night Live,* Film: *It's Pat!, God Said "Ha!"*) as a nun waiting for an appointment with Samantha's oncologist

"Q"-uotes

"What've you got against honeymoons? It's basically sex with room service."—Samantha

"I'm in the woods in my negligee and my cell phone only has two bars left. Help!"—Miranda

"It feels good to be sarcastic."—Miranda

Episode Four: "Out of the Frying Pan"

Q-tastic Trivia

Filmed at a time when a cabbie won't go to Brooklyn. Times have changed, and so have the per-mile rates.

Charlotte and Harry adopt Elizabeth Taylor Goldenblatt. *E!* strikes again.

The Men

Character	Actor	Slept with	Notes	You might know him from such gay-friendly films and shows as
Vincent	Jonathan Hadary		Tries a variety of ill-fitting and bad wigs on Samantha	1990: *Gypsy*

Q-gasmic Guest Star

Dana Ivey (*Oz, Home Alone 2,* Broadway: *Sunday in the Park with George*) as Trudy, a woman who gifts Charlotte with her less-than-show-worthy dog

"Q"-uotes

"I can't move to Brooklyn. Even cabs won't go there."
   —Miranda
"My hair is my thing."—Samantha
"Oh my God. I'm married."—Miranda

Episode Five: "The Cold War"

"Q"-uotes

"That dog's getting cruised more than me and we're on the corner of Gay and Gay."—Anthony
"You can take me out of Manhattan, but you can't take me out of my shoes."—Miranda

The Men

Character	Actor	Slept with	Notes	You might know him from such gay-friendly films and shows as
Tom	TR Pescod			

"Once the gay rumors start, it means you're really a
   star."—Samantha

"How can they just assume I'm gay?"—Stanford

"In the blink of a tabloid I went from Demi to Liza."
   —Samantha

"You'd think with all these faggy little dogs there'd be at
   least one horny circuit, muscle gay here. No. Nothing
   but boxy, thick-legged ladies and tweedy old
   queens."—Anthony

Episode Six: "Splat!"

Q-gasmic Guest Stars

Kristen Johnston (*Third Rock from the Sun*, Broadway:
   The Women) as Lexi, a former party girl who falls out
   a window, signaling the end of everyone's carefree
   days

Wallace Shawn (*The Princess Bride*, *Desperate
   Housewives*, *The L Word*) as Martin, a food critic
   Carrie introduces to Enid

The Men

Character	Actor	Slept with	Notes	You might know him from such gay-friendly films and shows as
Pet Store Guy	Tom Deckman		Recognizes that Elizabeth Taylor Goldenblatt isn't fat, she's pregnant	

"Q"-uotes

"Maybe in the other republics people like to share vibrators, but this is America, land of plenty."
  —Samantha

"We're selfish bitches who like you in New York."
  —Samantha

"Ladies, time's up. I can't pretend to be one of the boys any longer."—Stanford

Episode Seven: "An American Girl in Paris (Part Une)"

"Q"-uotes

"I'm going to miss you, you cunt."—Samantha
"Go get our girl."—Miranda

SEX AND THE SIDEBAR

I used to have all of the seasons on DVD and I watched them with alarming, if not addictive, regularity. During my time living in San Diego though, I lived with two boyfriends (not at the same time) and went through two traumatic breakups (not at the same time) with both. As upset as I was over the loss of love, security, and companionship, I was even more upset with my mysteriously disappearing *Sex and the City* DVD collection. Now I only own three seasons. I lost various things in my gay divorces—art, kitchen electronics, clothes—but the one thing I miss the most are my damned DVDs!

—JL, Johannesburg South Africa, Financial Advisor and Wine Connoisseur

Episode Eight: "An American Girl in Paris (Part Deux)"

Q-gasmic Guest Star

Carole Bouquet (not particularly well known on this side of the pond, but with a name like "Bouquet" and an air of breezy yet haute couture sophistication how can we not love her?) as Juliet, Aleksandr's ex-wife

The Men

Character	Actor	Slept with	Notes	You might know him from such gay-friendly films and shows as
Colorist	Steven Lock			
Paul	Julien Rouleau		Gay, French bookshop clerk who helps throw a dinner in Carrie's honor	

"Q"-uotes

"I'm gonna shoplift just so he can feel me up."—Anthony

"In your movie, how big is my part? Bit or supporting?"—Anthony

"A relationship is like couture. If it doesn't fit perfectly, it's a disaster."—Juliet

CHAPTER EIGHTEEN

The Finale Controversy

We couldn't help but
wonder . . .
was it good for you?

THE PROBLEM with ending a great television series, especially at the height of its popularity, is that you're probably never going to satisfy all of the viewers. When the announcement of the end of the show was made, fans immediately began speculating about what they thought would happen, and what they wanted to happen. Get Charlotte a baby. Don't let Samantha die. Have Miranda let down her defenses and embrace family life. Let Carrie and Big get back together. Actually, wait, keep them apart. No, they belong together. No they don't. Yes they do. The tension was palpable. What would the writers do? Would they, one way or another, finally provide closure to this relationship? Would this story, like traditional fairy tales, end with our heroine getting the guy? Would she finally realize that they just don't belong together? And what was she going to wear?

And many wondered about the ultimate question: would the series be left open-ended to be really—and we mean it this time—concluded in a movie?

Well, as fate would have it, we got our wishes. Or most of them, depending on what you wished for. But regardless of that, we were all absolutely delighted that the ending of the series found our girls older, wiser, and ultimately true to themselves.

Despite their prior disappointments, Charlotte and Harry received a photo, from their adoption agency, of the Chinese baby they were destined to adopt. Hugs and tears all around for our favorite optimist's unstoppable determination and persistence.

Not only did Samantha not die from her breast cancer, but perhaps more importantly she did not say "I love you" to Smith, who surprised her by returning early from filming his new Gus Van Sant movie. Kisses and slaps on the back for our favorite broad for surviving her illness and for not compromising with Smith or in this case, for not tearing down the wall shielding her heart.

Miranda, now living in Brooklyn, opens her home and her heart to Steve's mother, Mary, who, after a stroke, is now suffering from dementia. After Miranda searches the streets of Brooklyn for Mary, she brings her home and bathes her. Magda, on behalf of us all, bends down and, if not gently, then meaningfully, kisses Miranda on the forehead, saying "You love." True to character, Miranda remains silent, choosing instead to nod, in awkward acknowledgement. We get the sense that her life, though not necessarily what she thought it would be, is hers, and that she treasures it.

Big faces his, well—biggest—challenge when Charlotte brings him in front of the firing squad that is Miranda and Samantha, who finally accept the fact that he cares about Carrie, and tell him to "go get [their] girl" back from Paris.

When he arrives in Paris to rescue Carrie from her ill-conceived relationship with Aleksandr, Big finds that she's already rescued herself. That's our girl! We knew it would happen. After watching her take a backseat to Aleksandr's work and needs, we knew the time would come when she'd find herself again. And she did. The "Carrie" necklace she thought she lost was with her all the time, hidden in the lining of her clutch. It just took some time for the necklace, and Carrie's own self, to work its way out to the light again.

Carrie and Big get back together in Paris, Carrie and the girls are reunited at the coffee shop, and in the very last scene, on the streets of New York, we learn that his name is John. He has a name. We have closure. And with the following quote from Carrie, the show fades to memory:

". . . the most exciting, challenging, and significant relationship of all is the one you have with yourself. And if you find someone to love the you you love, well, that's just fabulous."

So, if you had been hoping for six more years of Carrie trying to find Mr. Right, you were disappointed, but if you were glad that Carrie arrived in the stable emotional place to explore a meaningful and committed relationship with someone with whom she has a deep connection, you were satisfied. If you were hoping for Big to have a more exotic name, like Cosmo, you were disappointed, but if you were pleased that his name was as ordinary as any other, perhaps indicating that despite all the drama over the past six seasons, he's just a man, you were satisfied. And if you thought Carrie should have tried to make it work with Aleksandr, you were disappointed, but if you wanted her to return to the city, and the friends, that she loved, the people and the places that were as much a part of her as she was of them, then you were satisfied. Of course, if you were hoping for Samantha to die, for Charlotte to never have children, and for Miranda to lose everything in a fire, then I have seriously misread you.

It's safe to say that the only disappointment each and every one of us can agree on was the glaring omission of Stanford in the final episode! What happened to our favorite gay pal? I guess we'll have to wait for the movie. And speaking of the movie . . .

CHAPTER NINETEEN

The Movie

We couldn't help but wonder . . .
would we ever see Samantha going down on the World-wide Express Guy in our local Cineplex?

THE ROAD to Hollywood, as we saw during Carrie's meeting with Matthew McCanaghay, is not an easy one. Though there was very strong interest around Hollywood, New York, and everywhere in between about a feature-length theatrical film taking up where the *Sex and the City* series left off, the project seemed to stall as quickly as the buzz started.

None of us will ever know the real reason for the project's demise, though most people tend to believe the reports that attributed it to strife among cast members. Perhaps that was the reason, but we also knew that like any family or friendship worth its salt, any differences could be worked out, and things would be set right. And we were right!

By early 2007, most, if not all, of the cast had officially signed on to reprise their roles, and pre-production, in the form of location-scouting and costume and scene designing was well under way.

In New York, the summer of 2007 will go down in history as the Summer of Sex, as cast and crew were spotted filming throughout the city. Print and television media, to say nothing of blogs and online sources, provided the citizenry of The City with daily, if not hourly updates on which actress was where and what she was wearing. Entertainment news programs devoted outrageous amounts of time to still photographs or man-on-the-street videos of a pregnant Charlotte chastising a forlorn-looking Big as her water breaks, to images of Carrie in an over-the-top wedding dress, and to shots of Miranda's new hairdo.

But what do we really know about the content of the film? Not so much. Scripts are on a complete lock-down, and it appears that cast and crew have signed confidentiality agreements so airtight it would take a miracle, or at least a night filled with Cosmos, to get a snippet of actual information from them. But, because I know you're dying to know, here's what I can tell you so far:

In addition to the entire cast returning, they'll be joined by Jennifer Hudson, the ex-*American Idol* contestant who won the 2007 Academy Award for Best Supporting Actress for her role as Effie White in *Dreamgirls*. She'll play Carrie's personal assistant.

According to Kristin Davis, not all the scenes being filmed are true. Dream sequences? False leads to throw off the press and public? Possibly, though probably both.

According to Kim Cattrall, the movie finds Samantha, who has to face the harsh reality of turning fifty, very bronze and very blonde thanks to all the time she's been spending in Los Angeles. Wonder if she ever gets invited back to the Playboy mansion.

According to Cynthia Nixon, Miranda will face the last thing in the world she thought she'd ever have to deal with. Well, we've already seen the new haircut, so that can't be it. Life without Magda? Will Brady turn gay?

According to Sarah Jessica Parker: Carrie's apartment is the beginning, middle, and end of the story. Make of that what you will.

What's sure to be true, however, is a huge opening weekend. Which brings us to the last issue . . . which Manolo Bahlniks does one wear to opening night?

Acknowledgments

Please join me in raising a Cosmo to the following, who were of invaluable help and support during the writing of this book: My all-too-trusting editor Joseph Pittman, who had Charlotte-like faith in my ability: my agent, Mitchell Waters, who has Miranda-like protection over my career: the men and women whose Samantha-like openness allowed them to contribute their real-life tales and insights: and my friends and family, too numerous to name, for their support, especially during my Carrie-like moments of neurosis, doubt, and the search for the perfect outfit.

They are all fabulous.